I had the distinct pleasure of knowing and being somewhat of an adopted spiritual son of Jack's. From my early days of knowing Christ to my latter years, Jack was my mentor and guide. Much of what you will read in this book is very much how Jack lived and how he taught others to live.

Jack lived in awe of the Bible, but more in awe of its Author. Jack believed that what the Holy Spirit led men to write all those many years ago is still fully applicable in current days. Jack strongly believed the Bible was to be taken literally in all of its 66 books. His dedication to meticulous research was the hallmark of this wonderful book.

If you have wanted to find a way to really grow in your knowledge of the Bible, I would strongly recommend that you spend time reading and studying Jack's book. You won't be disappointed.

Edward C. Hiers
CEO, Northeast Planning Associates
https://northeastplanning.com

How beautiful that the book, *Helping You Understand the Bible*, starts with "Why should anyone study the Bible and the importance and blessings of studying the Bible. The authors sharing their methods of studying the Bible is encouraging and a great example. None in this world is without problems. No solution to any problem can be found in this world. The authors beautifully and strongly establish that the Word of God is the only solution to every problem. This point leads people to study the *Bible* carefully.

Judy and Jack establish the fact strongly that the Author of the *Bible* is God Himself. It is so beautiful that they establish the fact that salvation or the born- again experience is the basic requirement to understand the *Bible*. In this book only we can see the role of the Holy Spirit in teaching the Word of God. It is very interesting to know that Satan does not like a regular *Bible* study. We can't find these kinds of facts anywhere else, which makes this book a special and meaningful one.

Listing 23 topics attracts anyone to start a topical *Bible* study. I appreciate the emphasis of meditation of the Word of God which is the central and important part of studying the Word of God. Filling the mind with God's Word, memorizing the scriptures, speaking the Word, and practicing the Word are wonderful revelations from the Holy Spirit and precious lessons for a diligent *Bible* reader.

I am pretty sure that the diligent reader of this book not only will be blessed himself, but will become a great blessing to others, also, by becoming an effective *Bible* teacher. This book surely will equip many *Bible* scholars. I praise Almighty God for giving outstanding knowledge and wisdom to the authors, Jack and Judy Hartman.

> **Pastor Ebenezer Moses**
> **President, India Gospel Fellowship**
> **Founder, Shepherds Council of India**

. God's Toolbox Series .

Helping You Understand the Bible:

God's Plan Made Clear

Jack Hartman & Judy Hartman

Lamplight Ministries, Inc.

Concord, North Carolina

Helping You Understand the Bible

Lamplight Ministries, Inc.
4258 NC Highway 49 S, #202
Harrisburg, NC 28075

Website: https://lamplight.net Email:
lamplightmin@protonmail.com
https://linkedin.com/judithahartman
Blog: https://lamplightmin.wordpress.com
Biblical health blog: https://judyannhartman.wordpress.com

ISBN: 978-0-91-544590-5
ISBN: 978-0-91-544591-2 E-book

Dedication

I dedicate this book to Dr. Gideon Tandirerung. Gideon, I want to thank you for being a man who has trusted God through the storms of your life. I compare you to Paul. From teaching Leadership Training to top executives in Indonesia to support your ministry to arriving in New York with your family, you have always started and pastored a church for Indonesian speaking people. In Miami where you fried donuts at 2 a.m. to support your family to arriving in Canada to settle as a refugee family, you always started and pastored a church.

I thank God for bringing us together, even though we have never met in person. You exemplify intellectual excellence being led by the Holy Spirit. Whenever I come across something in the *Bible* where I want an explanation, I contact you. You have a knowledge of the *Bible* that, I believe, imparts God's heart.

God has given you an extraordinary gift of teaching. I thank you and your dear wife, Claire, for returning to your home country of Indonesia and re-connecting with both church and government leaders who knew you and respected you so highly.

I thank you for serving as Southeast Asia Director of Lamplight Ministries, Inc. I thank you for preaching and teaching the love of God in Christ Jesus all across Indonesia as you lead seminars on Lamplight books, especially *Trust God for Your Finances*. Thank you for answering the call of God to take the gospel of Jesus Christ to Indonesia and the surrounding islands and countries.

Thank you for being God's instrument in faithfully spreading His Word which is *"a lamp unto our feet and a light unto our path.* (Psalm 119:105).

I so look forward to the day we meet in person!

Judy Hartman

Contents

Helping You Understand the Bible

Foreword

I have known of Lamplight Ministries, Inc. for many years and the Hartmans personally almost as long. Meeting them through the ministry changed my life. Through my privilege of reading many of their books, my life as a Christian and as a minister began to gain both depth and breadth.

I began to do more and more; become involved in more and more ministries; discovered the meanings of Scripture which increased my desire to learn, explore, and look inward. The Scriptures truly began to live in me. It was a journey that (through Jack and Judy) I knew would not end until my last day. It was exciting, daunting, and, above all, life-changing.

That is one reason why this book is important to every Christian, young or old, to the curious heart, to those searching and to the lost-those yet to receive the redemption waiting for them. There are numerous texts, courses, and other materials available today, but none that teach the heart, feed the spirit, or change lives like this book. It is one of many. It is one great resource for getting personal with Scripture and with God, and is the one book I recommend for those wanting to grow close to God and learn the fullness of salvation-how they were redeemed by the blood of Christ.

Read this book, use it, and make sure to share with others the name of this book. I can never thank Lamplight enough-Judy today, and the entirety of the ministry she and Jack shared with me.

Wesley B. Rose, Ph. D
"Dr. Ley" Light of Christ
Ministry/Scripture Institute

Preface

Dear Reader: I am excited for you to journey through this book whose primary purpose is to "get you into the Word of God, the *Bible*, and get the Word of God, the *Bible*, into you." As you will learn, every book in the *Bible* imparts God's Son, Jesus Christ, to you. Our goal in writing this book, if you have not met Him yet, is to introduce you to Jesus Christ, the Savior Who took your sin upon Himself, so that you can live in the presence of our heavenly Father. The most important decision you will ever make in life is to surrender your life to Jesus Christ. We explain the glorious gift of salvation through Jesus Christ in the section, —The Most Important Decision You Will Ever Make in Life at the back of the book. Do go there now if you have not begun your beautiful journey of knowing Jesus Christ and inviting Him to come and live in your heart and be Lord of your life. If you are already living for and serving our Lord Jesus Christ, we trust that your journey through this book will bring you closer to Him and ignite you to be increasingly bolder in sharing your faith in Christ Jesus as you grow in your knowledge of Him in His Word.

Jack wrote *How to Study the Bible* in 1985. It has been one of our most requested books over the years, next to *Trust God for Your Finances*. Therefore, I decided to update the book, but I left Jack's remarkable method of studying the *Bible*. You will be ever so grateful that you live in this time of the Internet and really wonderful *Bible* study websites. You will see how painstakingly Jack pursued the study of a topic and how he laboriously used a number of *Bible* reference books. Today, you have the Internet, so research is streamlined immensely. Jack never touched a computer. You have access to so many *Bible* study tools on the Internet today. Be thankful for them!

You will see what Jack wrote and how I did my best to weave our writing together and add many more *Bible* truths. Jack and I wrote one or two books a year for 29 years with five years spent writing ten sets of Scripture cards on specific topics. I am preparing these Scripture cards to be published again, so be watching for their arrival!

Can you imagine a husband and wife, each with an office at either end of the house, both at home all the time and co-authoring books? Both with a love for God in Christ Jesus and His Word and both with a passion to present Jesus Christ to hungry hearts, we made a great team. Being focused on the Word of God created such peace in our home.

As I explain in more detail later in the book, Jack was absent from the body and present with the Lord on September 17, 2018. At age 88 on no medications and with no specific ailments, Jack moved into eternity with Jesus Christ peacefully at home.

Since I know Jack's heart and vision so well, I am able to continue Lamplight Ministries, Inc. with the assurance that Jack would endorse what I am doing and what is taking pace in and through Lamplight Ministries, Inc.

Preface

I'm excited for you to meet Jack through this book, if you didn't already know him. I enjoyed adding tips that I believe will bless you. So, I'll pray for you right now: 'Dear heavenly Father, I thank you that this reader is seeking to know how to study your Word, the *Bible*. I pray that You will plant in this reader's heart a hunger and a thirst to know You and to know Your Word, the *Bible*. I "...do not cease to give thanks for you, making mention of you in my prayers; that the God of our Lord Jesus Christ, the Father of glory, may give to you the spirit of wisdom and revelation in the knowledge of Him, the eyes of your understanding being enlightened; that you may know what is the hope of His calling, what are the riches of the glory of His inheritance in the saints, and what is the exceeding greatness of His power toward us who believe, according to the working of His mighty power which He worked in Christ when He raised Him from the dead and seated Him at His right hand in the heavenly places, far above all principality and power and might and dominion, and every name that is named, not only in this age but also in that which is to come." (Ephesians 1:15-21).

Enjoy your journey through this book. I ask you with all my heart to contact me and to let me know if this book has made a difference in your life. I'll be looking to hear from you!

What you need to do right now is to go to our website and download for free the audio spoken by Jack himself in 1985 on How to Study the Bible! This is pure gold! (https://lamplight.net)

Jack and Judy

Introduction

Jack: Most Christians and many non-Christians try to study the study the *Bible* at one time or another, only to give up in despair a few days or a few weeks later because they are confused and frustrated. The *Bible* seems very complicated, but it really is not. In this book my primary goal is to show the reader a definite, workable and easily understandable system for studying the *Bible*.

I have referred to five different versions of the *Bible* in this book. For purposes of simplicity and clarity, the following abbreviations have been used:

NKJV – *New King James Version*
AMP – *The Amplified Bible*
NLT – *New Living Translation*
NAS – *New American Standard Bible* NIV – *New International Version*

This book is written for three groups of people:

First, this book is for anyone who has recently received Jesus Christ as his or her Savior. You are babies in the spiritual realm and your spiritual "milk" will come from studying the Word of God. "Like newborn babies, crave pure spiritual milk, so that by it you may grow up in your salvation, now that you have tasted that the Lord is good." (I Peter 2:2-3, NIV)

Second, it is written for people who have been Christians for some time, but never have been able to get into a consistent program of study and meditation in the Holy *Bible* – the Word of God. I pray that the clear, concise method outlined in this book will be the *Bible* study system that you have needed since you first became a Christian.

Third, I believe that this book will be read by many people who have not yet accepted Jesus Christ as their Savior. I pray that this book and its companion book, *One Hundred Years from Today*, will help you make the decision to receive Jesus as your Savior and start on an eternity of glorious spiritual growth, meaning and fulfillment.

Judy: Jack left this world on September 17, 2018. He was —absent from the body and present with the Lord. (II Corinthians 5:8) I know. I was there. Jack's son, Mike, and my daughter, Melissa, and I were standing around his bed. The night before, Kem, the nurse who volunteered to give Jack a bath each week, a *Bible* teacher who became instant family, had played a song as we were singing to Jack around his bed. The song was the Ray Boltz song: "Thank You for Giving to the Lord. "

With my hand placed on Jack's heart, I had been praying verses from Psalms and Revelation to Jack and thanking him for our beautiful life together. Jack's heart was pumping nicely. Mike and Melissa came into the room. Melissa played the song, "Thank You for Giving to the Lord" again. The final verse is: "I know that up in

Introduction

heaven you're not supposed to cry. But I am almost sure there were tears in your eyes as Jesus took your hand and you stood before the Lord. He said, My child, look around you, for great is your reward." At the very moment of the last note of the song, Jack's heart stopped beating.

Mike, Melissa, and I shared that moment. We will never be the same. We all experienced Jack's passing from this life to the next, —absent from the body and present with the Lord.

Jack was 88, took no medication, had no diseases, no pain ever. I took him on his daily car ride into the beautiful North Carolina countryside on Wednesday. The next Tuesday he left us. Jack's passing could not have happened more beautifully, wondrously, and gloriously.

I had to tell you, because I am writing this book through tears, because I am writing by myself, without Jack, for the first time. He is still the co-author of the book, because he first wrote it in 1985. You will be able to tell what parts I am writing and what parts Jack wrote.

Jack and I spent almost 30 years dividing the *Bible*, the Word of God, into bite-sized pieces in easy-to-understand language. Jack had an office at one end of our ranch style home in Dunedin, Florida. I had an office at the other end of the house. In the early years, Jack called me "red" and "scratch," because of all the red marks I would place on his writing and all the parts I would scratch out! Over the years we came to a remarkable harmony as we presented each biblical topic to "get the Word of God into people and get people into the Word of God. "

My primary reason for updating this book, which is one of the most in demand books we have written, is because Jack focused on one way to study the *Bible*. We were like night and day in our approach to studying the *Bible*. Therefore, I am adding the ways that I study the

Bible. I am certain that when you arrive at the end of this book, you will identify the ways that you prefer. I am also certain that over your lifetime, you will use many of them.

Your journey in the *Bible* is life-long. The *Bible* is like no other book on earth. It is alive. The words are living. You will spend your life exploring the depths of this message from God. You will find that the more you dig, the deeper the wellspring of the Word of God becomes to you. My prayer is that as you dig, your hunger to know God our Father through His Son Jesus Christ in the *Bible* will become unquenchable!

What you need to do right now! Go to our website, https://lamplight.net and listen to the free download of pure gold: Jack himself speaking to you from 1985 on How to Study the Bible. You will hear Jack's loving voice with every fiber of his being appealing to you to get to know our heavenly Father through His love letter to you, the *Bible*. Do it now! Jack's in heaven, but you can hear him now!

My prayer for you is that you will see Christ Jesus on every page. I pray that you will have a hunger and a thirst to devour the *Bible*, the Word of God, using both of our study styles. They are a perfect balance.

"Father, I pray that the dear reader will see You, meet You, and spend his or her life growing in knowing You. I pray that as we study Your Word, the *Bible*, together, that You will impart to each of us, the magnificence of worshipping You, beginning now and continuing throughout eternity. In the name of Jesus I pray. Amen. "

CHAPTER ONE

---•◦•◦•---

Every Word in the Bible Comes from God

J ack: At the age of 43, I found myself on the verge of bankruptcy and a complete emotional breakdown. I could not sleep at night. I worried constantly. There did not seem to be any way out but, by the grace of God, I found the answer that I had to have.

When I hit rock bottom, a friend from Oklahoma told me that there was only one way out and that was to let God solve my problems. He explained why I needed to accept Jesus Christ as my Lord and Savior and I did. (See the Appendix of this book to invite Jesus Christ into your life right this minute. Also, see Jack's book, *One Hundred Years from Today*, for a delightful account of Jack's journey with Jesus Christ.)

Then my friend said the words that led me on the path that has changed my life and the lives of many others. He said, —Jack, you have read many, many books written by men and women, *but you have never read the Bible – the one Book that is written by God*. Every word in that Book is inspired by God Himself and the only way you'll ever get out of this mess is to *saturate* yourself in that Book, learn what it says and then do it.

Jack and Judy: Every *Bible* study program should be based upon the foundation that the *Bible* is the Book with God inside it. When we study the *Bible*, our Creator talks to us. He gave us this Book as a means of daily contact with Him. He gave us this Book to instruct us, correct us and give us definite guidelines to follow.

"The whole Bible was given to us by inspiration from God and is useful to teach us what is true and to make us realize what is wrong in our lives; it straightens us out and helps us do what is right. It is God's way of making us well prepared at every point, fully equipped to do good to everyone." (II Timothy 3:16-17 TLB).

We should approach the *Bible* each day with awe and reverence, with the attitude that God and His Word cannot be separated. We should spend our time in God's Word daily exactly the way we would treat God Himself if He came to us each day and spent time with us, because He, indeed, does.

The Word of God tells us everything that we will ever need to know about how to live our lives here on earth. The reason why the *Bible* contains so much information about life is that the *Bible* has the same Author that life does. The more we learn from the *Bible*, the better we will get to know the Author.

This is the one Book that will absolutely *transform* our lives if we know what it says, believe what it says and do what it says to do. The apostle Paul explained this to the Thessalonians when he said: "… when you received the message of God [which you heard] from us, you welcomed it not as the word of [mere] men but as what it truly is, the Word of God, which is effectually at work in you who believe [exercising its superhuman power in those who adhere to and trust in and rely on it]. (I Thessalonians 2:13 AMP).

What is the message of God of which Paul speaks? The message in every book of the *Bible* is salvation through the Son of God, Jesus Christ. The author of the following account of Jesus Christ in every book of the *Bible* is unknown: 'Old Testament: in Genesis, Jesus Christ is the seed of the woman; in Exodus, He is the Passover Lamb; in Leviticus, He is our high Priest; in Numbers, He is the pillar of cloud by day and the pillar of fire by night; in Deuteronomy, He is the prophet like unto Moses; in Joshua, He is the captain of our salvation; in Judges, He is our judge and lawgiver; in Ruth, He is our kinsman Redeemer; in 1st and 2nd Samuel, He is our trusted Prophet; in Kings and Chronicles, He is our Reigning King; in Ezra, He is the rebuilder of the broken-down walls of human life; in Esther, He is our Mordecai; in Job, He is our ever-living Redeemer; in Psalms, He is our Shepherd; in Proverbs and Ecclesiastes, He is our Wisdom; in the Song of Solomon, He is the loving Bridegroom; in Isaiah, He is the Prince of Peace; in Jeremiah, He is the Righteous Branch; in Lamentations, He is our weeping Prophet; in Ezekiel, He is the wonderful four-faced man, in Daniel, He is the fourth man in life's "fiery furnace;" in Hosea, He is the faithful husband, forever married to the backslider; in Joel, He is the baptizer with the Holy Ghost and fire; in Amos, He is our burden-bearer; in Obadiah, He is the mighty to save; in Jonah, He is our great foreign missionary; in Micah, He is the messenger of beautiful feet; in Nahum, He is the avenger of God's elect; in Habakkuk, He is God's evangelist, crying, "revive their work in the midst of the years;" in Zephaniah, He is our Savior; in Haggai, He is the restorer of God's lost heritage; in Zechariah, He is the fountain opened up in the House of David for sin and uncleanness; in Malachi, He is the Sun of Righteousness, rising with healing in His wings;

New Testament: in Matthew, He is King of the Jews; in Mark, He is the Servant; in Luke, He is the Son of Man, feeling what you feel; in John, He is the Son of God; in Acts, He is the Savior of the world; in Romans, He is the righteousness of God; in I Corinthians, He is the Rock that followed Israel; in II Corinthians, He is the Triumphant One, giving victory; in Galatians, He is your liberty-He sets you free; in Ephesians, He is the Head of the Church; in Philippians, He is your joy; in Colossians, He is your completeness; in 1st and 2nd Thessalonians, He is your hope; 1st Timothy, He is your faith; in 2nd Timothy, He is your stability; in Philemon, He is your benefactor; in Titus, He is truth; in Hebrews, He is your perfection; in James, He is the Power behind your faith; in 1st Peter, He is your example; in 2nd Peter, He is your purity; in 1st John, He is your life; in 2nd John, He is your pattern; in 3rd John, He is your motivation; in Jude, He is the foundation of your faith; and in Revelation, He is your coming King.'

"For what is our hope, or joy, or crown of rejoicing? Is it not even you in the presence of our Lord Jesus Christ at His coming? For you are our glory and joy." (I Thessalonians 2:19-20). The *Bible* and this book are written so that you will be in the presence of our Lord Jesus Christ at His coming. Please share this book with everyone you love. The importance is eternal. This life is fleeting.

"Two little lines I heard one day, Traveling along life's busy way, bringing conviction to my heart, And from my mind would not depart. Only one life, twill soon be past.

Only what's done for Christ will last. Only one life, yes, only one, Soon will its fleeting hours be done. Then, in that day my Lord to meet And stand before His judgment seat. Only one life, Twill soon be past. Only what's done for Christ will last. Only one life, the still small voice Gently pleads for a better choice Bidding me selfish aims to leave, And to God's holy will to cleave. Only one life to lead. Twill soon be past. Only what's done for Christ will last. Find on the Internet C. T. Studd's poem, "Only One Life" for the remaining six verses.

You'll want to add biographies of God's great generals into your studies. Get to know men, such as C. T. Studd, who as a wealthy young man and a star English cricket player devoted his life to taking the gospel to China, India, and, finally, central Africa. He was the first missionary to reach many tribes deep in the Congo. His motto was: "If Jesus is God and died for me, then no sacrifice can be too big for me to make for Him."

Study missionaries, such as John Wesley (Europe and America), George Whitfield (United States), William Carey (India), Adonirum Judson (Burma), Jim Elliot (Ecuador), George Muller (orphanages in England), David Livingston (Africa), Hudson Taylor (China), and Loren Cunningham (YWAM-Youth with a Mission, world-wide) (I, Judy, am a YWAM Crossroads Discipleship Training School (CDTS) graduate, the training program for people over 30. See https://ywam.org, young or older, for a great adventure!

God's Word gives us everything that we'll ever need. It is overflowing with His great and precious promises to us. If we believe deeply in these promises and act in faith on them, we will take part in God's divine nature and escape the problems caused by evil desires.

"His divine power has given us everything we need for life and godliness through our knowledge of him who called us by his own glory and goodness. Through these he has given us his very great and precious promises, so that through them you may participate in the divine nature and escape the corruption in the world caused by evil desires." (II Peter 1:3-4 NIV).

We live in a very corrupt world. However, if we continually study and meditate in God's Word and fill our minds and hearts with His great, precious promises, we will have the spiritual strength needed to escape the temptations of our corrupt world.

We must recognize the need to feed ourselves spiritually just as much as we recognize the need to feed ourselves physically. "... Man shall not live and be upheld and sustained by bread alone, but by every word that comes forth from the mouth of God." (Matthew 4:4, AMP).

The key word in this verse is the word "every". We are not told that we should feed ourselves with only a few of God's promises. We are told that we should sustain ourselves by every word that God has given us. Clearly, we are called to a lifetime of study and meditation in God's Word in order to receive the continuing spiritual strength and energy that we need.

In the physical world, we repeatedly eat breakfast, lunch and dinner and this food is transformed into physical *energy*. In the spiritual realm, when we feed ourselves regularly with spiritual food from God's Word and then act on it by continually speaking it with our mouths and living by it in our lives, we produce the spiritual strength and energy that is called *faith*.

We would not expect to live well in the physical realm on one or two meals a week, yet this is exactly what many of us do in the spiritual realm! Many of us hear the Word of God once or twice each week and that's "it" for us. If we just partake of spiritual food once or twice each week, we won't have the spiritual strength and energy needed to survive the crisis times of life.

Instead of just "nibbling," we need to "feast" on the Word of God. If we do, our hearts will overflow with joy from the spiritual strength and energy that will surge through us. "Your words were found, and I ate them; and Your words were to me a joy and the rejoicing of my heart ..." Jeremiah 15:16, AMP).

In the natural realm, honey tastes good. In the spiritual realm, the Word of God tastes much better. The more we taste the wonderful Word of God, the more we'll understand it. As a result, we will be able to stay off the dark roads of life which will eventually cause us serious problems. "How sweet are your words to my taste, sweeter than honey to my mouth! I gain understanding from your precepts; therefore, I hate every wrong path." (Psalm 119:103-104, NIV).

God's Word is a seed. "... The seed is the word of God." (Luke 8:11, KJV). In the natural world, we would not expect to reap if we did not sow. We should not expect this result in the spiritual realm, either. If we continually plant the seed of God's Word in our minds and hearts, we will experience a bountiful harvest.

Our Father has given us a rule book to live by and a map to guide us every step of the way. This combination rule book and map is His Word. When we're at a crossroads and don't know which way to go, God's Word will show us. "This is what the Lord says: 'Stand at the crossroads and look; ask for the ancient paths, ask where the good way is, and walk in it, and you will find rest for your souls...'" (Jeremiah 6:16 NIV).

What would we think if friends were coming to visit us and they arrived several hours late, because they thought they knew the directions, but never checked the GPS for specific directions? This is not very intelligent, is it? Yet, isn't this exactly what many of us do? Many of us think that we're good Christians, but we travel down many wrong roads and we're confronted with many problems in our lives simply because we haven't continually studied the directions that our Father has given to us.

God's Word is like a bright light. The more we study it, the more we will see and comprehend spiritual concepts that were previously unclear to us. "The entrance and unfolding of Your words give light; their unfolding gives understanding (discernment and comprehension) to the simple." (Psalm 119:130 AMP).

Non-Christians are in spiritual darkness. They stumble and don't know why. We were in darkness, too, but we came out of it and into the light when we became Christians. We can continue to walk in this light if we stay on the path that God has laid out for us. "... you were formerly darkness, but now you are light in the Lord; walk as children of light..." (Ephesians 5:8 NAS).

If we continually study and meditate in God's Word, we will see our way more and more clearly and we won't stumble as we go down the road of life. "The path of the righteous is like the first gleam of dawn, shining ever brighter till the full light of day. But the way of the wicked is like deep darkness; they do not know what makes them stumble." (Proverbs 4:18-19 NIV).

God's Word is a lamp that casts light on the road of life. "Thy word is a lamp unto my feet, and a light unto my path." (Psalm 119:105 KJV).

We need to follow the explicit, precise instructions that our Father has given us. If we do, no matter how fast the pace gets, we won't stumble. "When you walk, your steps will not be hampered; when you run, you will not stumble. Hold on to instruction, do not let it go; guard it well, for it is your life." (Proverbs 4:12-13 NIV).

We can't begin to comprehend how pure and clean life can be until we live in complete obedience to the magnificent, purified Word of God. "The word and promises of the Lord are pure words, like silver refined in an earthen furnace, purified seven times over." (Psalm 12:6 AMP).

The purity of God's Word has been tried and proven true again and again. It will shield us if we will trust it. "Every word of God is tried and purified; He is a shield to those who trust and take refuge in Him." (Proverbs 30:5 AMP).

God's precious promises belong to us. If we study and meditate on them continually, they will *cleanse* us. "… since these [great] promises are ours, beloved, let us cleanse ourselves from everything that contaminates and defiles body and spirit …" (II Corinthians 7:1 AMP).

In addition to being pure and clean, God's Word is *supernaturally alive and full of spiritual power and energy.* If we immerse ourselves in it continually, it will pierce to the very center of our personality. It will go into our hearts. If

9

something bad is buried there from childhood or other times in the past, God's Word will identify the problem and show us how to cure it:

"For the Word that God speaks is alive and full of power [making it active, operative, energizing, and effective]; it is sharper than any two-edged sword, penetrating to the dividing line of the breath of life (soul) and [the immortal] spirit, and of joints and marrow [of the deepest parts of our nature], exposing and sifting and analyzing and judging the very thoughts and purposes of the heart." (Hebrews 4:12 AMP).

God's Word has enormous supernatural power. Its power will break down and consume anything and everything that might harm us. "Is not My word like fire [that consumes all that cannot endure the test]? says the Lord, and like a hammer that breaks in pieces the rock [of most stubborn resistance]?" (Jeremiah 23:29 AMP).

The depth of God's Word is amazing. It is full of spiritual treasures. The more we dig, the more highly we will value it. The more we learn, the more we'll be aware of how little we know "...Oh, the depth of the riches of the wisdom and knowledge of God! How unsearchable his judgments, and his paths beyond tracing out!" (Romans 11:33 NIV).

No other book can even begin to compare with the *Bible*, because no other author can even begin to compare with the Author of the *Bible*. God's thoughts are amazingly profound. "How great are your works, O Lord, how profound your thoughts!" (Psalm 92:5 NIV).

I, Jack, have studied and meditated continually in the Word of God since July 20, 1974, and I haven't even come close to scratching the surface of it. Many people have studied the *Bible* every day for 30, 40, 50 and more years and have never come close to comprehending everything in this wonderful Book. Who else but God could have written a Book that we can never get enough of? What other book can we study month after month, year after year and never stop learning from it?

I, Judy, by God's grace, have studied the *Bible* all my life, since I was a child attending the San Marino Community Church in San Marino, California. I enjoyed categorizing verses, memorizing verses, and noting verses in a small notebook. Today I carry three by five cards with verses on them, a habit introduced to me by Jack. Every day God opens new meaning of the Scriptures to me. The *Bible* is the only book in the world that was not written in the world. It was inspired from heaven; thus, it is filled with wisdom that is gleaned and never fully mastered in a lifetime. It is a deep pool that has no bottom. The greatest joy is opening the *Bible* each day to see what God says to me to empower me for the current day's assignment from Him.

We will never outgrow the Word of God. It is in a class by itself. All the answers are in there, just waiting for us to find them, understand them and act in faith on them. We can't approach the limits of this Book, because there are none. The more we comprehend the *Bible*, the more we will see that God will open new spiritual horizons to us.

God's Book is vastly different from any other book. Most books last only a few years and are then forgotten. The very best books written by men and women have lasted for a few hundred years. God's Book has stood the test of time. Parts of it were written more than three thousand years ago. This Book will never fade – it will last forever. "...man is like the grass that dies away, and all his beauty fades like dying flowers. The grass withers, the flower fades beneath the breath of God. And, so it is with fragile man. The grass withers, the flowers fade, but the Word of our God shall stand forever." (Isaiah 40:6-8, TLB).

The Word of God is eternal. It will last longer than heaven or earth. "Heaven and earth will pass away, but My words shall not pass away." (Matthew 24:35 NAS).

God's instructions will always be there to guide us "...the Word of the Lord [divine instruction, the Gospel] endures forever..." (I Peter 1:25 AMP).

The eternal, unchanging truth of God's Word is not affected in the least by recession, depression, unemployment, sickness, wars or any other conditions of this world. God's promises give us the permanence and certainty that we need in these rapidly changing times.

When God's Word says something, we *can* depend on it *completely* because "... it is impossible for God to tell a lie ..."(Hebrews 6:18 TLB).

God's promises never fail. "... there hath not failed one word of all his good promise ..." (I Kings 8:56 KJV).

God's Word is the rock-solid foundation that we need. "... God's truth stands firm like a great rock, and nothing can shake it. It is a foundation stone ..." (II Timothy 2:19 TLB.

Nothing can compare with the value of learning from the Word of God. "Receive my instruction, and not silver; and knowledge rather than choice gold. For wisdom is better than rubies; and all the things that may be desired are not to be compared to it." (Proverbs 8:10-11 KJV).

Our Father has given us complete instructions for every area of our lives. We'd better pay close attention to what He has told us. "A wise son heareth his father's instruction ..." (Proverbs 13:1 KJV). We are foolish if we do not listen. "A fool despiseth his father's instruction ..." (Proverbs 15:5 KJV). Learning how God instructs us to live our lives, we will experience for ourselves that the Word of God is truly a lamp unto our feet and a light unto our paths.

Judy: I will present historical evidence of the validity of the *Bible*. First, the validity of the birth of Jesus Christ. Regarding Josephus, a Jewish historian (AD 37-AD 100) we find: In Rome, in the year 93, Josephus published his lengthy history of the Jews. While discussing the period in which the Jews of Judaea were governed by the Roman procurator Pontius Pilate, Josephus included the following account: "About this time there lived Jesus, a wise man, if indeed one ought to call him a man. For he was one who performed surprising deeds and was a teacher of such people as accept the truth gladly, He won over many Jews and many of the Greeks. He was the Messiah. And when, upon the accusation of the principal men among us, Pilate condemned him to a cross, those who had first come to love him did not cease. He appeared to them spending a third day restored to life, for the prophets of God had foretold these things and a thousand other marvels about him. And the tribe of the Christians, so called after him, has still to this day not disappeared."
(See http://josephus.org/testimonium.htm.

Detailed biographies of eyewitnesses of Jesus Christ date from around 40 years after He died: the biblical gospels of Matthew, Mark, Luke, and John. The letters of Paul were written within 25 years of the death of Jesus Christ.

The *Bible* has 66 books, 39 books in the Old Testament and 27 books in the New Testament. These 66 books were written by 40 different authors from all walks of life: fishermen, doctors, farmers, tentmakers, prophets, priests, and kings over a period of 1,500 years. It was written in Hebrew, Aramaic, and Greek.

As the *Bible* was copied over the years, the agreement of the copies with the original is remarkable. For instance, of the 643 copies of Homer's *The Iliad*, there is 95% agreement, according to the Christian and Apologetic Ministry website. The New Testament has 6,000 known Greek manuscripts. The agreement is 99.5%. The degree of difference in agreement in the copies of the writings of Plato, Aristotle, Caesar, and Homer ancient classics, is greater than the degree of difference in agreement in the ancient manuscripts of the *Bible*. (lifehopeandtruth.com)

Let's look at the historical evidence of the crucifixion of Jesus Christ. The authors of the four gospels were actual historical people in history who gave eyewitness accounts of the crucifixion of Jesus Christ.

The death of Jesus Christ was never disputed. (https://allaboutjesuschrist.org/historicalevidenceofthec rucificion-fac.htm) Darkness covered the land for three hours. (See Matthew 27:45; Mark 15:33; Luke 23:45) The crucifixion of Jesus Christ is covered in all four gospels. (Matthew 27:33-44; Mark 15:22-32; Luke 23:33-43; John 19:17-30) Let's look at the historical evidence of the resurrection of Jesus Christ. In the *Bible*, Jesus Christ was seen after His resurrection by at least seven of His followers. (Mark 16:14; Luke 24:33-37; John 20:19-20; Acts 1:3) He was also seen by 500 people. (I Corinthians 15:3-7) An earthquake occurred. (Mallet, 1853; Rigg, 1941)

14

Simon Greenleaf (1783-1853), an American attorney, an expert in judicial review, wrote *The Testimony of the Evangelists.* He gives accounts of the life of Jesus, His ministry, His death, and His resurrection, testimonies that would be accepted as evidence in a court of law even today. Thousands upon thousands of martyrdoms, the remarkable spread of Christianity, and faith through persecutions unto death serve as proof that Jesus Christ was God, that He lived, died, and rose from the dead and lives today. (See whatchristianswanttoknow.com/historicalevidenceofjesus-christs-resurrection/) Twenty-eight prophecies were fulfilled on Resurrection Day. (See https://cbcg.org/franklin/SA/SA_28prophecies.pdf)

We remember that there are 66 books in the *Bible*: 39 books in the Old Testament and 27 books in the New Testament. Every Old Testament book is quoted in the New Testament, except Esther, Ecclesiastes, Song of Solomon, Ezra, Nehemiah, Obadiah, Nahum, and Zephaniah. There are 400 years between the Old and New Testaments. There are 300 quotes from the Old Testament found in the New Testament, including partial quotes. Jesus quoted from 24 different Old Testament books. (https://Bible.ca)

"You can shut Him up for a fool, you can spit at Him and kill Him as a demon; or you can fall at His feet and call him Lord and God. But let us not come up with any patronizing nonsense about His being a great human teacher. He has not left that open to us. He did not intend to." (C.S. Lewis, Cambridge University)

CHAPTER TWO

---•◆•---

The Foundation for
Understanding God's Word

We have seen *why* studying the Word of God is so important. So, we have a hunger to know everything we possibly can about our Father's plan for us, His history and what is yet to come, and what He instructs us to be and do. So, now, we need to consider *how* to study His precious Book, the *Bible*.

We must realize that spiritual rebirth is necessary in order to understand the Word of God. Satan, the god of the world, blinds the eyes of people who are not reborn spiritually so they cannot understand the amazing truths in God's Word. "If the Good News we preach is hidden to anyone, it is hidden from the one who is on the road to eternal death. Satan, who is the god of this evil world, has made him blind, unable to see the glorious light of the Gospel that is shining upon him, or to understand the amazing message we preach about the glory of Christ, who is God." (II Corinthians 4:3-4, TLB).

We cannot understand the Word of God until we have experienced spiritual rebirth. In order to really understand God's Word, we must have received the fullness of the Holy Spirit who is our Father's gift to us. We need to *ask*

Him for this gift. "...how much more shall your heavenly Father give the Holy Spirit to them that ask Him?" (Luke 11:13, KJV). We are equipped! "...out of his glorious, unlimited resources he will give you the mighty inner strengthening of his Holy Spirit." (Ephesians 3:16 TLB).

The same Holy Spirit who had the mighty power to raise Jesus from the dead lives inside of us if we have elected to become a child of God through Jesus Christ. "...the Spirit of God, who raised up Jesus from the dead, lives in you..." (Romans 8:11 TLB). He will guide us in every area of our lives – especially in studying and obeying the Word of God.

God's Word is the truth. "...Your Word is Truth." (John 17:17 AMP). Jesus told His disciples that, after He had ascended into heaven, the Holy Spirit, the Spirit of Truth, would come and that He would guide us to all truth. "...when He, the Spirit of Truth (the Truth-giving Spirit) comes, He will guide you into all the Truth (the whole, full Truth) ..." (John 16:13AMP).

Our Teacher, the Holy Spirit, lives inside of us. He is with us all day long, every day of our lives, and is there to teach us God's great truths. He is able to guide us into areas of comprehension of God's Word that are beyond our fondest dreams. "... The man who is not a Christian cannot understand and cannot accept these thoughts from God, which the Holy Spirit teaches us. They sound foolish to him, because only those who have the Holy Spirit within them can understand what the Holy Spirit means. Others just cannot take it in. But the spiritual man has insight into everything, and that bothers and baffles the man of the world, who cannot understand him at all." (I Corinthians 2:14-15 TLB).

The Holy Spirit is within us to impart God's heart to us. "...the thoughts of God no one knows except the Spirit of God. Now we have received, not the spirit of the world, but the Spirit who is from God, that we might know the things freely given to us by God, which things we also speak, not in words taught by human wisdom, but in those taught by the Spirit, combining spiritual thoughts with spiritual words." (I Corinthians 2:11-13 NAS).

The Holy Spirit makes the *Bible* come alive to us. See again II Timothy 3:16: "All scripture is given by inspiration of God..." Every word in the *Bible* was inspired by God. The Holy Spirit is inside us to open to us the truths of the *Bible.*

The *Bible* is more than one book. It is a Library consisting of 66 different books by 40 different authors, written on three continents in three different languages over a period of 2500 years. The *Bible* is the living Word of God. (Hebrews 4:12)

The *Bible* seems dull to many people. The *Bible* was written as the history of God's plan. Since the Holy Spirit gives understanding of the *Bible*, He is not present in the lives of anyone who is not a child of God. Therefore, the *Bible* will be difficult to understand for people who have not surrendered their lives to Jesus Christ as their Lord and Savior and, thus, received the Holy Spirit into their lives.

Each day ask the Holy Spirit to reveal the truths of the *Bible* to you as you spend time with your heavenly Father reading, studying, and meditating upon His Word. "Open my eyes, that I may behold wondrous things out of Your law. I am a stranger and a temporary resident on the earth; hide not Your commandments from me." (Psalm 119:18-19 AMP).

God answers prayer. Our job is to pray. "And whatever you ask for in prayer, having faith and [really] believing, you will receive." (Matthew 21:22 AMP).

Prayer has some requirements: (a) pray in line with the Word of God (b) leave the answer to God. "This is the confidence we have in approaching God: that if we ask anything according to his will, he hears us. And if we know that he hears us – whatever we ask – we know that we have what we asked of him." (I John 5:14-15 NIV).

The Holy Spirit will guide us to understanding the truth of God's Word. As we study diligently, He also will cause us to want to obey the instructions that we receive. "... I will put my Spirit within you and cause you to walk in My statutes, and you shall heed My ordinances, and do them." (Ezekiel 36:27 AMP).

The *Bible* is so clear! First, in order to be able to understand the truths of God, we must be reborn spiritually. Second, we need to accept by faith that the Holy Spirit – the Spirit of Truth – lives inside of us. Third, we should turn quietly and confidently to the Spirit of Truth each day and ask Him to guide us as we study the *Bible*.

Studying God's Word each day is essential in order to *renew* our minds, to *change* our thought processes, so that we will think, speak and act more and more the way that God thinks, speaks and acts. The ways of this world are very different from God's ways. His thoughts and His way of doing things are on a much higher plane than men's thoughts and ways. "For my thoughts are not your thoughts, neither are your ways my ways, saith the Lord. For as the heavens are higher than the earth, so are my ways higher than your ways, and my thoughts than your thoughts." (Isaiah 55:8-9, KJV).

Our Father has provided instructions for us. He gives us warnings. He gives us the answers we need. "(Do not be conformed to this world (this age), [fashioned after and adapted to its external, superficial customs], but be transformed changed) by the [entire] renewal of your mind [by its new ideals and its new attitude], so that you may prove [for yourselves] what is the good and acceptable and perfect will of God, even the thing which is good and acceptable and perfect [in His sight for you]." (Romans 12:2 AMP).

Most of us renew our bodies each day with breakfast, lunch and dinner. We also renew ourselves each night when we sleep. Most of us realize the importance of renewing our bodies in order to keep them in good physical condition. Of even greater importance is to renew our minds and keep them in good spiritual condition.

We all grow older with each day that passes. God's Word tells us that we can offset the aging process of the outer man by continually renewing the inner man, by restoring him and keeping him refreshed at all times. If we do, we'll remain strong within ourselves by the power of God in Christ Jesus and we won't be worn down by worry and fear. "... we do not become discouraged (utterly spiritless, exhausted, and wearied out through fear). Though our outer man is [progressively] decaying and wasting away, yet our inner self is being [progressively] renewed day after day." (II Corinthians 4:16 AMP).

We are instructed to renew our minds each day.

However, many Christians fail in this area. Why does this happen? One reason is that Satan comes hard against us when he sees us starting on a continuing, daily program to renew our minds in the Word of God. Our mind is his battlefield. Filling our minds with the Word of God protects us. Satan is a thief. His plan is to steal the precious inheritance that we have received from Jesus Christ. "The thief comes only to steal and kill and destroy..." (John 10:10 NIV).

Remember Satan's goals. Our Father has given us a Book of Instructions that tells us everything that we'll ever need to know in order to defeat Satan. If we are going to manifest the glorious victory that Jesus has given us, we need to study this Book continually in order to live in victory.

How can we expect to live in victory if we don't take time to study in detail the Book of Instructions that God has provided? However, this is exactly what many Christians do and this is exactly what Satan's goal. We will be strengthened spiritually if we renew our minds in God's Word each day. If we identify our weak areas and meditate upon God's Word especially in these areas, we will win the battle for the mind. We will increase daily thinking God's thoughts. "And now, dear brothers and sisters, one final thing. Fix your thoughts on what is true, and honorable, and right, and pure, and lovely, and admirable. Think about things that are excellent and worthy of praise." (Philippians 4:8 NLT).

"... the word of God abideth in you, and ye have overcome the wicked one." (I John 2:14 KJV). Be on guard. As God's Word starts to get down into our hearts, Satan comes immediately and, in any way that he can, tries to take God's Word out of our hearts before it has a chance to take root. "… Satan cometh immediately, and taketh away the word that was sown in their hearts." (Mark 4:15 KJV).

We have a powerful weapon, the Word of God. "…by the Word of Your lips I have avoided the ways of the violent (the paths of the destroyer)." (Psalm 17:4 AMP).

God tells us to be prepared and equipped with the Word of God. "…he that is begotten of God keepeth himself, and that wicked one toucheth him not." (I John 5:18 KJV).

As soon as we plan a regular, scheduled time of worship and praise of God with study and meditation upon His Word, we will be bombarded with distractions. If we set a time with God and keep it for 28 days, we have created a pattern. If we continue for 90 days, we have created a habit. Time with God must be scheduled on our calendars and be the most important appointment of the day.

We'll never find time to study God's Word. We have to *make* time! We need to put our time with God first ahead of everything else. The daily goal is to get to know our heavenly Father. We get to know someone by spending time with him. We must learn our Father's way of doing things and then to obey these instructions.

Now that we have laid the foundation for a regular program of *Bible* study, we're ready to get into specifics – exactly how to study the *Bible*. We must start with a strong desire to learn our Father's instructions and a definite commitment to stick to this program on a daily basis. Plan to meet with God for 28 days at a certain place at a certain time with a *Bible*, notebook or computer, and be ready to take notes from God. A good way to start is to get dressed, drink a glass of pure water with one or two tablespoons of

Bragg's Organic Apple Cider Vinegar (to alkalinize your body) or lemon juice. Then continue to sip pure water as you begin your time with God.

In case you missed it! Now, that you've become acquainted with the legend, Jack Hartman, here's what you need to do, Go to our website, (https://lamplight.net) and listen to or download for free Jack himself speaking to you from his heart on why you must get to know our heavenly Father in Christ Jesus through spending time in the *Bible.* Go now!

CHAPTER THREE

———◆•◆•◆———

Starting a Specific Program of Bible Study

Now that we have laid the foundation for a regular program of *Bible* study, we're ready to get into specifics – exactly how to study the *Bible*. We must start with a strong desire to learn our Father's instructions and a definite commitment to stick to this program on a daily basis. Know that creating a habit is not easy. Be determined to persevere.

The crucial period is the first few months. This process gets easier as the months pass, because our good habits can be made to work *for* us in the same way that our bad habits work *against* us. The more we get into the habit of studying and meditating in God's Word daily, the stronger the habit will become and the harder it will be for us to break it.

Are you determined to start a program of renewing your mind through studying and meditating in God's Word daily? Are you able to persevere against the distractions that you know will come? If you are, we now ready to start on a specific, detailed program of *Bible* study.

I'm going to assume that each reader of this book has never followed a regular program of *Bible* study. Those of you who have can adjust accordingly. I'm going to recommend specific *Bibles*. (Jack preferred *The Amplified Bible* because it does what it says, amplifies. Today the *Bible* I, Judy, prefer is the *New King James Bible*.) Jack gave the 1985 prices for the *Bibles* he recommended. Today you can easily find prices for the *Bibles* on the Internet.

Let's focus on the original source of the *Bibles* we are using. We recommend for the Old Testament sources, the Masoretic Text and for the New Testament the Textus Receptus. The Masoretic Text was preserved by Levitical scholars known as the Masoretes from about 500 A.D. to 850 A.D. They preserved the work of Aaronic priests and Levitical scribes, guardians of the Hebrew text, appointed by Ezra, the prophet. The source is https://biblicalarchaeology.org.

There are four basic types of *Bibles*: word-for-word (formal equivalence); meaning-for-meaning (closest natural equivalence); thought-for-thought (functional equivalence); and paraphrase (retelling). The commonly used word-for-word *Bibles* are: *New American Standard Bible (NASB), English Standard Version (ESV), New English Translation (NET), King James Version (KJV),* and *New King James Version (NKJV).* The meaning-for-meaning translation is *God's Word* translation. The thought-for - thought translations are: *Christian Standard Bible (CSB), New International Version (NIV),* and *New Living Translation (NLT).* The paraphrase translations are: *New International Reader's Version (NIRV), The Message (MSG),* and *God's Word Translation (GNT).* The source is https://godsword.org.

If a new Christian came to me and asked exactly what to purchase in order to start a systematic program of daily *Bible* study and meditation, I would advise starting with two *Bible*s – the *New King James Version,* published by Thomas Nelson Bibles, and *The Comparative Study Bible,* published by Zondervan Bible Publishers. Purchase a sturdy *Bible* that will last a long time, if possible. These *Bibles* are available on smile.amazon.com (assuming you have chosen a charity to bless). (We recommend carrying paperback copies of the *New King James Bible* with you to give to anyone you meet who does not have a *Bible.*)

A comparative *Bible* we recommend includes side by side for *comparison* the *New International Version* (NIV), the *New King James Version* (NKJV), the *New Living Translation* (NLT) and *The Message Bible* (Message). You will have one word-for-word translation, two thought-for-thought translations, and one paraphrase translation of the *Bible* to use in your biblical research, study, and meditation.

Another comparative study *Bible* we recommend includes side by side for comparison the *New International Version* (NIV), the *King James Version* (KJV), the *New American Standard Bible* (NASB), and the *Amplified Bible* (AMP). You will have two word-for-word translations, one thought-for-thought translation, and one amplified *Bible.* We recommend purchasing both comparative *Bibles.*

Jack: My *Comparative Study Bible* is my most valued possession. If I was told that I could keep only one item that I own and this —something could not be duplicated at a later date, it would not be our home, our automobiles, our financial assets or anything else. I would take *The Comparative Study Bible,* which is more valuable to me than any other possession. I use it on several occasions almost every day of my life. I can't imagine living without it.

Let's take a brief look at the four different versions of the *Bible* that are contained in one of the Comparative Study *Bibles*. The *King James Version* is the standard. It was translated in England approximately 400 years ago. It has stood the test of time and has been widely accepted by Christians for many, many years.

The *Amplified Bible* is a Literal Equivalent translation that, by using synonyms and definitions, both explains and expands the meaning of words in the text by placing amplification in parentheses, brackets, and after key words. This unique system of translation allows the reader to see the meaning as it was understood in the original languages. The result is an *Amplified Bible* that is easier to read and better than ever to study and understand. The *Amplified Bible* of 2015 includes more amplification in the Old Testament and refined amplification in the New Testament.

The *Amplified Bible* amplifies the *Bible* for us. *Webster's New World Dictionary* says that the word "amplify" means "to develop more fully." A group of *Bible* scholars spent many years in research and study of many versions of the *Bible* and then carefully amplified it with various shades of meaning, always being certain that their expanded version remained true to the original Hebrew and Greek.

The *New American Standard Bible* is an updated translation of *The American Standard Version* of the *Bible* which was published in 1901. This 1901 version received wide acceptance and a large group of *Bible* scholars reviewed, modernized and updated it in the 1960s. I have found it to be an excellent translation.

The *New International Version* is a contemporary English translation of the *Bible* that was made by over a hundred *Bible* scholars who diligently studied Hebrew and Greek texts. This group consisted of participants from many different denominations. They spent many thousands of hours working to provide accurate translation which is also clear and understandable. I believe that this is also an excellent translation.

The beauty of *The Comparative Study Bible* is that the reader can open it to any page and *see all four of the translations side by side*. *The King James Version* (KJV) and *The Amplified Bible* (AMP) are side by side on the left-hand page and *The New American Standard Bible* (NASB) and *The New International Version* (NIV) are directly opposite side by side on the right-hand page. If you purchase both comparative study *Bibles,* you will have seven different *Bible* translations to compare.

How I rejoiced when this *Bible* was published! It is tremendous having these four translations parallel to one another. This *Bible* has greatly increased my understanding of the Holy Scriptures and I'm confident that it will be of great benefit to anyone who is seriously interested in learning more from the Word of God.

This parallel *Bible* is my most valued possession. If I was told that I could keep only one item that I own and this "something" could not be duplicated at a later date, it would not be our home, our automobiles, our financial assets or anything else. I would take *The Comparative Study Bible* which is more valuable to me than any other possession. I use it on several occasions almost every day of my life. I can't imagine living without it.

I turn to *The Amplified Bible* more than any other. The amplification is magnificent and has given me a much better understanding of the Word of God. When *The*

Amplified New Testament first came out, Dr. Billy Graham said that it was "...the best study testament on the market. It is a magnificent translation. I use it continually."

I, Judy, use both of the *Comparative Study Bibles*, so I see seven translations! I am so very grateful to the people who spent years creating these Study *Bibles*.

Another *Bible* that serious *Bible* students should consider is the *Thompson Chain Reference Bible*. It features a numerical chain reference system. Dr. Frank Thompson spent over 30 years exhaustively grouping Scripture verses into chains and putting numerical references throughout the *Bible* for thousands of verses of Scripture. Because of this, the reader can go to the topical listing in the back of the *Bible* and see other verses of Scripture under the same topic, as well as a listing of similar topics.

The next item that any serious *Bible* student should purchase is a *Bible* concordance. I don't see how anyone can seriously study the *Bible* without one. A concordance is a book that lists every word in the *Bible* in alphabetical order. I use *Strong's Exhaustive Concordance* and the word "exhaustive" describes it perfectly. This book contains over 1500 pages. Every word in the *Bible* is included.

For example, the word "love" is used 304 times in the *Bible*. This concordance gives the Scripture verse for each of the 304 times that this word is mentioned, along with a numerical listing for looking up these words in the original Hebrew or Greek. This concordance is invaluable. I use it constantly. I don't believe that it is an option. It is a must.

A topical *Bible* is very helpful. If you have a chain reference *Bible*, you might feel that is sufficient. However, I have found a topical *Bible* to be valuable also. I use *Nave's Topical Bible*. A condensed paperback edition is available.

On the cover of my topical *Bible* is a quote from Dr. Billy Graham which says, "Outside of the *Bible*, this is the book that I depend on more than any other. Certainly, there has been no book that has helped me more in my study." This 1,464page book exhaustively lists topics and has many verses of Scripture on each topic. It is a wonderful study aid that offers numerous listings of Scripture verses on any topic imaginable. This, plus a chain reference *Bible*, connects the various topics of the *Bible* beautifully.

Another *Bible* study aid that is optional, but very helpful, is a *Bible* dictionary. If we don't understand the meaning of certain words in the *Bible*, this is where we can find the answer. A good *Bible* dictionary will assist us in comprehending and understanding many of the words, people and places referred to in the *Bible*.

I use *The New Compact Bible Dictionary*, published by Zondervan Publishing House. There are over one million copies of this dictionary in print.

This completes the listing of *Bible*s and *Bible* study aids that I personally believe are necessary to study the *Bible* effectively. Many other study aids are available – expository dictionaries, *Bible* commentaries, Greek-English lexicons, *Bible* handbooks and many more.

Now, let us take a look at what technology provides us for the study of the *Bible*. Today, when you want to know an exact verse and you can remember a few words of the verse, you can use a search engine online, such as duckduckgo.com. Put in the few words and click. The verse will appear. *Bible study became "instant!"*

I left Jack's method of study in the book, so you can see how many hours he spent researching the *Bible*. Jack never touched a computer, so these study *Bible*s were in constant use. Today, we can look up any part of any verse on the Internet and have it in a moment. We can see a list of all the verses relating to any topic in the *Bible* in a moment. Be thankful today for the Internet and how it serves us so very well for *Bible* study.

There are many different *Bible* applications that you can use as you study the *Bible*. I, Judy, use https://*Bible*gateway.com when I want to find a verse in any translation. I also use this website to listen to the *Bible* on audio. You will be totally blessed by going to https://blueletter*Bible*.org. You will find a tutorial explaining how the *Bible* study tools we have mentioned are all available for free. This website is excellent for in depth word studies showing the meaning of a word in the original language. Go to https://youversion.com/the-*Bible*-app/ and find wonderful study tools and *Bible* experiences as well. On https://*Bible*.is you can view "The Jesus Film" that has been shown all over the world to bring people to know and understand Jesus Christ Who came to set them free and bring them eternal life.

We are so blessed to live with today's technology! God has provided it for us to know and understand His Word in depth. The *Bible* study tools online make studying the *Bible* so easy.

Now that we have reviewed the basic "tools" that are needed to start a *Bible* study program, we're ready to put these tools to work. At this point I want to make it clear that *there is no one method of studying the Bible*. There are definite scriptural principles on how to study God's Word, but there are many different *methods*.

Studying the Bible by Topic

In the following chapters, Jack explains the specific method that he used to study and meditate in the Word of God: This method has worked very well for me, for students in our *Bible* study classes during the past ten years and for other people all over the world. I have received numerous letters commenting on this method. Let me share excerpts from just a few of these with you:

"Your method of study is neat and I will use it. Thanks for your refreshing, helpful and strengthening direction." (D.S. — Arizona)

"I am using your system of 3x5 cards daily. I study the *Bible* every morning about 1- 1/2 hours. I have outlined your system and I am using the study tools that you recommend. Your teaching is sound. It witnesses strongly to me." (D.H. — Ohio)

"I am indebted to you for opening the doors of my mind further than they have ever been before. I think of God constantly." (D.S. — Colorado)

"We are following the biblical principles which you out-lined and the Lord is blessing us in many ways." (R.S. — British West Indies)

"I'm following your suggestions on meditation and it is amazing to see how I can concentrate on God all day long instead of only once in a while." (G.B. — Canada)

"You have spelled the principles out so simply. I am now meditating in the Word daily. You did a great job." (D.K. — Georgia)

"I never could understand 'meditate day and night' but praise the Lord, I do now. Thank you and God bless you." (L.H. — New York)

We have other similar letters on file. I can guarantee you that this system does work!

For all my Christian life since age 42, I have studied the *Bible by subject*. This method helps us to overcome specific problems in any one area of our lives. Studying one book of the *Bible* can enrich us and studying *Bible* history can increase our understanding of the *Bible* as a whole. At one time or another in our *Bible* study, we should follow these methods. However, at the start, these methods may not help us to overcome problems in our lives to the degree that the subject method does.

I started using this method because of necessity. My *Bible* study started because I was on the verge of bankruptcy and an emotional breakdown. I avoided these problems by saturating myself in the Word of God and learning everything I possibly could about the instructions our Father has given us on these two specific subjects.

Not only did this work in my life, but I then taught on both of these subjects in the *Bible* study class that I teach. These *Bible* studies later became books, *Trust God for Your Finances* and *Deep Inner Peace*, which have helped many people all over the world.

For many years, I have taught a *Bible* study class on many different subjects. When I discovered the problems that were caused by my impatience, I studied what the *Bible* had to say on patience. I learned how to overcome anger, how to become more loving, how to appropriate the strength of God, how to increase faith and decrease fear, etc. Much of what I have learned has been shared with many other people and it has helped them.

I observe many people trying to study the *Bible*. They are reading it – one chapter after another after another –

with no goals in mind. I like to find answers in the *Bible*. I am focused on studying the *Bible* by topic, to solve major issues in life.

The *Bible* is not a theoretical book. *It is an immensely practical book.* Our Father gave it to us to show us how to deal with the everyday problems that we have to face. The *Bible* can be used effectively in each of our lives right now — today! No matter what our problems might be, God's Word has the answer.

If we learn how to use the subject method of studying the *Bible,* we'll find many specific answers to our problems. Continual study and meditation in a specific area will draw us closer and closer to the Author of these verses of Scripture. If we want to know someone well, we spend a lot of time with that person. If we want to know the Lord better, we need to spend a lot of time with the Book that He has written. His wisdom is available to us in any area where we need it.

Long ago, I learned that the first step in solving any problem is to define exactly what the problem is. A problem well defined is half solved. I ask each reader to stop right here and ask yourself, "What are my biggest problems? What are my specific goals? What subjects do I need to study in God's Word?" Define your specific problems and/ or goals and then to aim your *Bible* study in that particular direction.

I have compiled the following alphabetical list of typical problem areas that concern most of us at one time or another. Look over this list. Perhaps it will help you to decide what subject you need to study in God's Word:

1. Anger: I knew I got angry too often, so I studied this subject in detail. See all that God's Word has to say on this subject.

2. Children: Exactly what does the *Bible* teach us about bringing up children?

3. Faith: What exactly should we do to build stronger faith in God?

4. Fear: What specifically must be done to overcome fear in our lives?

5. Forgiveness: Most Christians know that we need to forgive others, but this is easier said than done. Why should we forgive someone who has hurt us very badly? How can we forgive?

6. God: How can we know Him better? Exactly what does His Word say about developing a closer relationship with Him?

7. Heaven (and hell): What is heaven really like? How can we know if we're going there? Is there really a hell? What is it like? Why would a loving God allow anyone to go to hell?

8. Healing: When we are sick and need healing, exactly what should we do? Jesus healed many people in His earthly ministry. Is healing still available today? Why are some people healed and not others?

9. Holy Spirit: Who is the Holy Spirit? What does it mean to be filled with the Holy Spirit? What exactly is required to release the power, love and wisdom of the Holy Spirit in our lives?

10. Jesus Christ: Some Christians really don't know Jesus Christ very well. Sometimes we hear people talking

about a close personal relationship with Jesus Christ. How can we get to know Him better?

11. Joy: Some of us need to know how to experience more joy and happiness in our lives. What does the *Bible* teach about how to experience more joy and happiness?

12. Love: Some of us are not as loving as we should be. If we want very much to be more loving, how is this accomplished?

13. Marriage: Some Christians have problems with their marriage. What does the *Bible* teach us about how to get along better with our spouse?

14. Patience: Some of us are impatient and we know that we need to become more patient. We might try and fail because we don't know how to develop more patience. What does God's Word say about this?

15. Peace: Some of us need to calm down and relax. Some of us are quite tense. How can we quiet ourselves and experience the peace of God?

16. Prayer: Some of us are not getting many answers to our prayers. We don't really know how to pray. Exactly what does the *Bible* teach about how to pray to God?

17. Pride (and Humility): Some of us are too proud, stubborn and self-centered. We'd like to overcome these traits, but we don't know how. How can we lick these problems and become humble?

18. God's All Sufficiency (and Money Management): Some Christians have financial problems and don't know how to solve them. What does the *Bible* teach us about overcoming financial problems?

19. Satan: What are Satan's ways to deceive? How can we live in wisdom and avoid Satan's snares?

20. Spiritual Growth: Some of us haven't experienced significant spiritual growth since we became Christians. We know that we need to grow more, but we need help.

21. Strength: Some of us are not as strong spiritually as we should be. When we're under pressure, we give in far too easily. We know that we need more strength, but we don't know how to develop it.

22. Witnessing: Some of our friends and loved ones are not saved. We don't want them to go to hell. More than anything else, we want to help them find Jesus Christ as their Lord and Savior. How do we share Jesus Christ with them?

23. Worry: Some Christians worry a lot. Some of us are always anxious about something. What does the *Bible* teach about overcoming worry and tension?

This list is not complete and some of the problem areas overlap. However, I believe that this demonstrates what I mean about identifying specific problems and goals. If you are interested in expanding to many other topics, you might be interested in other sources of topical information.

For an excellent source for topics, see our book, *What Does God Say?* We present 94 topics, including Heaven, Hell, Eternal Salvation, Adversity, Death, Faith in God, Fear of the Lord, Grace of God, Holy Spirit, Inadequacy of Human Abilities, Long Life, Morning Time with the Lord, Omnipotent, Omniscient, and Omnipresent God, Patience, Pride, Protection from God, Revenge, Satan, World-Turn Away From, Worry and Anxiety, Victory of

Jesus Christ, plus many that will fill your heart with God's wisdom and counsel. You will come to know God more intimately through 94 topics God presents to you in His Word, the *Bible*.

One group in Iowa has been using *What Does God Say?* for several years in their Sunday morning *Bible* class. The leader asks everyone how their week went. Then he looks over all the answers and selects the topic that most clearly covers the main issues of the week. The class reads that chapter together, emphasizing the Scripture verses.

The class discusses the chapter and prays together. Class members can put the key verses on three by five cards and keep them handy all week and pray them back to God during each day, making them personal and thanking God for this portion of His Word. *What Does God Say?* is a topical handbook that some people keep right next to their *Bibles*.

A special request to you to do the very next time you are on your computer! What a gift you will be giving to Lamplight Ministries, Inc.! Go to https://smile.amazon.com and put Lamplight Ministries, Inc. as the charity you are choosing. You only need to make this request one time. Thereafter, every single time you order on https://smile.amazon.com, amazon will donate a small percentage of your order to Lamplight Ministries, Inc.! That would be such a wonderful blessing. You just choose Lamplight Ministries, Inc. one time and from then on, you will be blessing this ministry every time you order on amazon.com. Make a note to remind yourself of this great gift you can give. We thank you so very much.

Before you go any further, please stop right here and put this book down. I ask each reader to prayerfully decide the areas where you need help. This might take you just a few minutes, but it should take longer. It could even take several days. *Before any of us start a Bible study program, it is important to know exactly what we need to study.* Too many people try to study the *Bible* without having any specific goals and they give up because it does not help them.

Have you *defined* the specific subject or subjects that you want to study? Once this has been accomplished, we are then ready to go ahead with a specific plan to study the *Bible* to solve these problems and accomplish these goals.

Make a plan as well to read through the *Bible* and a place to meet with God each day. Have your tools ready: pen, pencil, notebook, and your *Bible*. I like to use sticky notes for writing names or situations for prayer. My prayer room is in my closet. I sit with my back to the door that goes to the water heater and place sticky notes on my dresser which is right next to me. This plan came from the movie, "The War Room" that you will want to see, for certain, if you have not seen it, or even watch it again.

CHAPTER FOUR

---•◆•◆•◆•---

Studying a Subject in the Word of God

W e now have picked a specific subject of study in the *Bible*. We have the *Bible* study tools that we need. Now we're ready to use these tools in order to find the answers that we're seeking. How do we begin?

Before starting, we must know the difference between reading the Bible and studying it.

One time I was discussing this with my business partner, Ed Hiers, and he gave me an interesting comparison between reading the *Bible* and studying the *Bible*. He said that he could have a book titled *How to Survive When You are Lost in the Woods* and read it casually in his home. However, if he actually was lost in the middle of a large forest and had this book with him, he'd do much more than just read it. He'd *study* it. He'd *devour* it. *He would pay close attention to every word because his life would depend on it.*

Study the *Bible* as if your life depends upon it! Select a topic and devour all that you can find on your topic. Think about the topic and about how God is going to provide answers that you have been so hungry to find.

Think of studying the *Bible* as a journey you are taking, searching far and wide for the answer. God has the answer!

Every time you open the *Bible*, you are in a deep conversation with your heavenly Father! He is always there to listen to you and to talk with you. He will speak in the quietness of your heart as you learn to listen. (I John 5:14) You are on an adventure! Have your note pad or computer ready to take notes. Go on an amazing journey with God in His Word daily!

Every time you open God's Word, you will learn new truths. You will even gain new understanding of verses you have known for a long time. God's Word is a deep well that continues to reveal truth and truth to you as you search for it. "These things have I spoken to you, that in Me you may have peace. In the world you will have tribulations; but be of good cheer, I have overcome the world." (John 16:33)

II Timothy 2:15 has been my guiding light ever since I started studying the *Bible*. It tells us that we need to *study* God's Word diligently, *"rightly dividing"* God's Word to find each of His precious nuggets on whatever subject we might be studying. The Word is alive. God is very aware of your time that you spend in His Word, seeking to know Him more intimately. He is there to communicate with you every minute of every day. "Study to show thyself approved unto God, a workman that needeth not to be ashamed, rightly dividing the word of truth" (II Timothy 2:15, KJV).

We will focus now on "rightly dividing" God's Word. You will find this adventure a deep joy! You are studying God message to you, His child! What does "study" mean?

Webster's New World Dictionary says that to "study" means "careful attention to, and critical examination and investigation of, any subject, event, etc.; to apply one's mind to think attentively; try to learn or understand by reading, thinking, etc."

If anyone ever claims that the *Bible* is not for people of high intelligence, tell that person that the *Bible* was created outside of time and space and that it is timeless. (Watch "The *Bible* in 24 Hours" by Chuck Missler on https://youtube.com.) Explain that the *Bible* can only be understood by God's children, those who are His own. Tell that person that the *Bible* is foolishness to anyone who has not entered the kingdom of heaven through God's Son, Jesus Christ. (II Corinthians 2:14)

God instructs us to examine the *Bible* closely and to pay careful attention to what it says. He instructs us to dig, dig and dig some more, always searching for valuable bits of truth. He instructs us to reflect and think deeply about what He is saying to us in His Word. (Hebrews 4:12)

Every word in the *Bible* is inspired by God! The day will come when you will spend hours with God in His Word. If you have not seen the movie, War Room, you can see it for free on https://youtube.com. In this movie, you learn the value of having a specific room in your house or a specific area of your house that is set aside for prayer, which includes time in God's Word.

Now let's take an actual subject and go through it one step at a time. I have used this procedure with the subject of "patience," so we'll use this as our example. How can we learn what God's Word teaches about becoming more patient?

We should start by collecting *every* possible verse of

Scripture on this subject. The first thing I do is to get out a dictionary to find other words that go along with patience. *Webster's New World Dictionary* mentions the words "steadfastness," "endurance" and "perseverance" in its definition of patience. (Today you can do an Internet search for the meaning of each word.)

We now have expanded from one word to four. Our next step is to look up all possible verses of Scripture on these four words. In *Nave's Topical Bible* we find 35 different Scripture references under the subject of patience. At the end of those references we are also referred to the tops of "longsuffering" and "meekness." (Today you can do an Internet search for *Bible* verses on "patience.")

At this stage of developing our subject, I would recommend just listing for now the chapter and verse references for each of the 35 references. Don't copy the text of the Scripture yet because all of these references are in *The King James Version*. Once we have all of our Scripture references listed, we're going to look them up in *The Comparative Study Bible* and in *The Living Bible*. We'll then be able to look at five different translations for each verse before choosing the verses that we want to use. (You can enter the list into a file on your computer saved under *Bible* Study, if you prefer. Today, you can copy and paste verses from your favorite *Bible* website.)

Once we have the 35 references listed, we should then turn in our topical *Bible* to the recommended subjects of "longsuffering" and "meekness." We find nine references under "longsuffering" and 54 references under "meekness." These references also should be written on a list, eliminating all duplications of Scripture previously listed.

Additional references are also given at the end of "longsuffering" and "meekness." Each reader will have to decide just how far to go with these additional references. You'll soon find that you will have a *tremendous* number of verses of Scripture.

We still haven't done anything with our other words — "steadfastness," "endurance" and "perseverance." Looking these up in the topical *Bible*, we find nothing listed under "steadfastness" and "endurance," but both of these refer us to "perseverance."

When we look there, we find a "gold mine" of 66 Scripture references plus references to other topics. (If you go to www.blueletter*Bible*.org, you can do a word study there. You will save a lot of time! All of these study tools are available there.)

We should then list the chapter and verses of Scripture references, once again eliminating the duplicates. We're finished with the topical *Bible* for now. Next, we should go to the concordance and look up the same subjects.

We'll usually find that at least 90% of these Scripture references have already been listed. However, you will acquire a few additional verses. Next, if you have other topical references, follow this same procedure. When this is done, we are then ready to go to a chain reference *Bible* and look up each of the verses of Scripture that we have listed.

Judy: Technology has made *Bible* study so much easier. You can use the books separately or you can to https://www.blueletter*Bible*.org and find these tools there to use more easily.

Be thankful that you live today! This older method of study was laborious and time consuming. Today you can see the results immediately. Today's technology is for God's people to use to study His Word. The tools that are available are beyond the imagination of people who studied in years past. Thank God every day for technology and pray that it will be used only for God's glory.

Here again is Jack's method of study: Each of us has to decide how many references we want to write down. Personally, I like to exhaust every possible resource. I often have at least a hundred references. On some subjects I have found several hundred references. Once we have all of these references listed, what do we do next?

I normally get out *The Living Bible* and *The Comparative Study Bible* and look up each of these verses of Scripture in five different versions of the *Bible*. As I do this, I leave out the references I don't want. I write each one I want to keep on a 3x5 plain file card or in a notebook, printing each of them neatly and carefully listing the Scripture reference and the version of the *Bible*. I also add any of my own comments or notes on the other side of the card or in a notebook. (It is important to only write on one side of the page in the notebook. You might want to cut up these notes and Scriptures to categorize them later, so you want only one side to have verses on it.

I, Judy, want you to see Jack's system of study so you can understand how blessed you are to be living today! Audio and digital books provide *Bible* study. I so enjoy listening to an audio *Bible* on https://.Biblegateway.com.

Be careful about the Christian books that you read! Some of them can mislead you. I always browse through a Christian book to make sure the author has used many

Scripture references, not an infallible gauge, but I'm not interested in a lot of personal opinions by an author. I'm only interested in Christian books that help me to understand God's Word better.

Discover if the book you are considering contains a lot of Scripture. Pray and ask for the Holy Spirit's guidance. If you feel led to buy a particular book, read it prayerfully and carefully. Most important is for you to know the *Bible,* so you will recognize when you read something that is contrary to God's Word.

You can listen to many different Christian pastors on https://youtube.com. Be careful about which pastor you choose. Only listen if you know that the *person* speaking presents the *Bible* correctly. We are told that in the last days there will be many false teachers. "For false christs and false prophets will rise and show great signs and wonders to deceive, if possible, even the elect." (Matthew 24:24) You can see the necessity of make every effort to know the *Bible,* so that you will recognize false teaching. Listen to the audio *Bible* whenever you can as well as read and meditate upon the *Bible.*

If your pastor broadcasts online, listen to each message again. Take notes and write *Bible* verses on three by five cards and carry them with you. Discuss what you learned from each message with your family and friends. Keep the message alive. Send your pastor a text or an email mentioning what how you were encouraged by the message.

Be careful about the television shows you watch. The Word of God can be perverted just slightly to lead you to trust not in God, but in something that takes your faith away from God. God instructs us to check everything we read, see or hear to see if it agrees with the Word of God. (II Corinthians 13:5)

We need to persist. We'll find a little bit here and a little bit there. We need to keep fitting the pieces together. It is thrilling and fulfilling to see all of these pieces from the Creator of the universe come together from many different sources. "For precept must be upon precept, precept upon precept; line upon line, line upon line; here a little, and there a little..." (Isaiah 28:10, KJV).

This system of *Bible* study is very similar to constructing a house. We start with a solid foundation — the Word of God. There is no more solid foundation than this! Then, we build on this foundation, one piece at a time, fitting the pieces together until they make a solid whole.

So far, we have only done one thing and that is to collect a large number of verses of Scripture on a particular subject that we have chosen. Our next step is to make some sort of correlation between all these verses of Scripture. I have completed this task many times.

Anyone who has followed our system will have many 3x5 cards on a given subject (or a notebook filled with pages of Scripture references on the same subject). The next step is to wait until we're fresh at the start of a new day of *Bible* study and then to pray, asking the Holy Spirit to guide us to "rightly divide" this subject.

Then, we need to get all our verses of Scripture and go through them, trying to label each with a subtopic – a title with just a few words. This will get all the material into workable categories for when we meditate on the Scriptures at a later time. If a few words that describe a portion of Scripture come to mind, write these words down. Continue this process until we have gone through every verse of Scripture that has been listed.

The best way to show you how to complete this process is to give you an example from the subject of patience. After I had looked up every possible verse of Scripture on the subject of patience, I went through the Scriptures I had copied and wrote out the following list of topical subheadings:

1. What does patience mean?
2. Why are so many of us impatient?
3. What does it mean "to take possession of our souls?"
4. How do we take possession of our souls?
5. How does patience relate to endurance?
6. How does hurry relate to patience?
7. How does worry relate to patience?
8. How can we calm down and slow down?
9. What does it mean to wait on the Lord?
10. How does pride affect patience?
11. Why is God's timing different from ours?
12. What is the relationship between prayer and patience?
13. How can we develop more endurance?
14. Patience is a fruit of the Holy Spirit. What is required for this fruit to be practiced in our lives?
15. What is the relationship between faith and patience?

16. What should we do when it seems as though we can't be patient any longer?

17. How can we keep our attention off the problem and keep it focused on Jesus?

Please do not be frustrated if you come up with an entirely different set of subheadings than I did. I have used this procedure several dozen times over the past years and I'll undoubtedly come up with many different subtopics than you will. (If you want to see this particular subject developed in its final form, listen to the audio on our website: "Taking Possession of Our Souls."

Methods will differ, but principles always stay the same. There are two principles here that we all should follow. First, collect all possible verses of Scripture on a specific subject using every conceivable source – topical, concordance, reference *Bible*, study *Bible*, books, audio, digital, etc. Second, once all these verses of Scripture have been collected, try to subcategorize at least to some degree.

As we go through this process, much of the material that we have accumulated probably will be discarded. Our goal is to find everything that we possibly can on a given subject and then to "whittle it down to size" — to get it into some kind of order.

This step finishes the "accumulation stage." Now that we have paid the price of hard work, digging out many verses of Scripture on a particular subject and doing the best possible job that we can of categorizing these verses under subtopics, we're ready to move on to the next step —meditating day and night on the Scripture that we have found.

Judy: To study the *Bible* today using the subject or topical method, go to www.blueletter*Bible*.org and complete a word study in a fraction of the time required using each separate *Bible* study tool to complete the word study. Again, be thankful that you live in today's world with technology that allows you to have *Bible* study by topic at your fingertips literally.

In case you missed it! Now that you know Jack better, what you must do now is to go to our website, https://lamplight.net, and for free listen to or download Jack's imparting to you his heart on why and how you must get to know God through studying the *Bible*. You will be so blessed by Jack speaking to you.

CHAPTER FIVE

Meditating on the Word of God

At this point, we have "collected" a great deal of scriptural material on the subject that we have decided to study. This consists of a big stack of 3x5 cards or a notebook filled with many pages of handwritten notes. Each of these cards or each numbered item in the notebook consists of a portion of Scripture with perhaps a few notes or comments. These have been grouped together into categories. To categorize the material in the notebook, simply cut up each item on every page and then group them. You may have compiled verses in an Excel file on your computer. You may have created a Word file to note the verses on a specific topic.

What do we do with this mess of information? The answer is to *meditate* on it. When we *study* God's Word, we *feed* ourselves with spiritual food. When we meditate on God's Word, we *digest* this spiritual food. If we have carefully followed the process that has been outlined, we have "eaten" a great deal of spiritual food. Now we need to learn how to digest it, so that we can put it to use.

The Word of God places tremendous emphasis on meditation. God's Word says that *we succeed by meditating on His Word day and night.* "This book of the law shall not depart from your mouth, but you shall meditate on it day and night, so that you may be careful to do according to all that is written in it; for then you will make your way prosperous, and then you will have success" (Joshua 1:8, NAS).

Let's study this verse of Scripture on meditation in detail and actually meditate on it — turning it over and over, looking at it from every angle to see how it applies in our own lives.

At the end of this verse of Scripture, God gives us His promise. He says that, if we meet the conditions of this verse of Scripture, we will be prosperous and successful. The Hebrew word that is translated "prosperous" means spiritual prosperity — prosperity in every area of our lives. Remember that success means to have exactly what we need when we need it to complete God's plan for our lives.

This verse of Scripture tells us that "this book of the law" (the Word of God) shall not depart out of our mouths. If something does not depart out of our mouths, this means that it is in our mouths continually. When we "meditate day and night" on a verse of Scripture, we need to open our mouths and speak this verse of Scripture continually – over and over and over again throughout the day and night.

Spiritual power is released by speaking the Word of God. In fact, the Hebrew word that is translated "meditate" in Joshua 1:8 actually means "to murmur" or "to mutter" – to speak the Word of God constantly. There is a very close connection between meditating in God's Word and speaking it continually.

Joshua 1:8 tells us to meditate on God's Word day and night. We have already seen that meditation means to speak God's Word continually. What else do we do when we meditate on God's Word?

My definition of meditation is "to reflect quietly, deeply and thoroughly on a subject over a period of time." When we meditate on the Word of God, we take one portion of Scripture and meditate on this throughout at least one day and night

Before we start this process, we should ask the Holy Spirit to cause this portion of Scripture to come alive. (John 14:26) We should ask Him to personalize it – to show us exactly how it applies to us and how it can be used in our lives. We should ask Him to expand this portion of Scripture – to show us new depth of meaning.

Most of us have jobs that require us to work eight hours or more each day. We also have family and church and community responsibilities. Because of these commitments, we obviously can't *study* God's Word throughout the day and night.

As I have mentioned in my previous books, God's Word tells us that the best time to *study* His Word is in the early morning. When we have finished our morning study on whatever the Lord leads us to study on this particular subject, then spend the *rest* of the day and night *meditating* on Scripture. We may not be able to study God's Word throughout the day and night, but we certainly can meditate on one portion of Scripture during that time.

We can meditate on a verse while we're showering, while we're driving to work, whenever possible while we're at work, on our breaks, on our lunch hour, when we drive home from work and during quiet time in the evening. At home we can meditate on specific verses of Scripture while cooking, cleaning the house, buying groceries, moving the lawn, or trimming the hedge.

Not only can we meditate throughout the day and night of our work week, but we have even more time to meditate on God's Word on weekends, holidays and vacations. If we stop to think about it, most of us have an abundance of time to meditate on the Word of God!

Continual meditation on the Word of God is the key that unlocks the door of success in our lives. Our Father instructs us to meditate on His Word throughout the day and night. You can see in Psalm 119 the power of God's Word. Throughout the *Bible,* you will find declarations about the power of the Word of God, but Psalm 119 has 176 verses proclaiming the magnificence of God's Word. "...seek for (aim at and strive after) first of all His kingdom, and His righteousness [His way of doing and being right], and then all these things taken together will be given you besides." (Matthew 6:33 AMP) One way to seek God with all our hearts is to meditate upon His Word. "My tongue shall speak of Your word, for all Your commandments are righteousness." (Psalm 119:177 NKJV). "—Unless Your law had been my delight, I would then have perished in my affliction." (Psalm 119:92 NKJV). "I will never forget Your precepts, For by them You have given me life." (Psalm 119:93 NKJV).

Some of us have our priorities completely backward. We're all caught up in the cares of the day when we should be putting God's Word in first place – far, far ahead of anything else that concerns us. See what happens when we put God first, especially first in the morning. "Blessed are those who keep His testimonies,
Who seek Him with the whole heart!" (Psalm 119:2)

Are we getting up in the morning to study the Word of God? Are we passing up precious moments when we could be meditating – while driving our automobiles, while exercising, while doing routine tasks which leave our minds free and when we have breaks during the day and night? Are we giving large amounts of time to meditation on God's Word? "Deal bountifully with Your servant, That I may live and keep Your word." (Psalm 119:17)

Let us discipline ourselves to take advantage of every minute of discretionary time. Some of us are passing up many opportunities. This is a "luxury" that we cannot afford. If we meditate continually on God's Word, our lives will be transformed! Give this system a fair trial and see for yourself.

Before getting into specific procedures for meditation on God's Word, I'd like to say one last word on the subject of meditating "day and night." Meditating on God's Word at night is key, especially just before we go to bed. What do many of us do instead? We watch some of the poor television or Internet programs that are on today and then top it off by watching the late news. What a way to prepare ourselves for a good night's sleep!

Some of us need to change our habits and cut down on the Internet or the television and cut out the late evening news. It can wait until morning – in fact, much of it can be ignored. Instead, we should spend a good amount of time each evening meditating on God's Word. This exercise is especially important just before we go to sleep. Many of us will sleep a lot better and we'll wake up much more refreshed. If we meditate on God's Word just before we go to sleep, our inner person can turn it over and over throughout the night while the outer person sleeps. This is extremely beneficial to us.

Now that we have laid the foundation for meditating on God's Word, let us get very specific. Exactly how do we go about meditating day and night? As with the study of the *Bible*, there is not any one method. However, I know that the method that I use works. So, let me show you this specific method of meditating on the Word of God.

Meditation is the *"bridge"* between studying God's Word and acting on God's Word. I believe that 3x5 file cards are excellent for meditation. The verse or verses of Scripture that we want to meditate on should be printed neatly on a 3x5 card. A few brief comments can be added on the other side of the card. If you copied the Scriptures on a computer or in a notebook, now is a good time to copy them on file cards for meditation.

We should keep this card with us for at least 24 hours. Men can carry it in their shirt pockets. Women can carry it in their purses. People working at home can keep it in front of them as they work.

Throughout the day, meditate on this Scripture every chance we get. Speak it out loud over and over and over. Pray, asking God, "Exactly how does this verse of Scripture apply to me? Show me how You want me to change, so that I can live my life more in accordance with the way this verse of Scripture tells me to live it."

This system works beautifully! There are no shortcuts. We should not try to rush it. We should not give ourselves "spiritual indigestion" by trying to gobble down more than one Scripture per day. We need to "chew" this slowly. We need to turn it over and over, think about it and personalize it. If we "only" do one verse of Scripture each day, we still will have meditated on 30 separate verses each month and more than 350 each year!

Chew our spiritual food slowly to digest it properly. We will receive maximum spiritual nutrition from each precious morsel.

CHAPTER SIX

---•+•+•---

Our Hearts – the Key to Our Lives

God's Word is not effective in our lives until we pay the price of getting it off the printed pages, into our minds and then down into our hears? The answer is to mediate continually on the Word of God.

Continual meditation in God's Word will cause the Holy Scriptures to become firmly established in our *minds*. As we *continue* to meditate, the Scripture *drops down into our hearts- the key to life*. Our lives center around *what we really believe in our hearts*. We should be willing to work diligently, each day meditating on God's Word, so that it will come alive in our hearts. Nothing is more important. "Keep your heart with all vigilance and above all that you guard, for out of it flow the springs of life" (Proverbs 4:23, AMP).

Memorizing verses of Scripture is a good start. There is a thin line of separation between memorizing and meditating. Memorizing can be done on the mind level without your whole being participating. For instance, I, Judy, am memorizing the Presidents of the United States. When I focus on memorizing the list by name, I can do it, but the list has far more meaning when I learn something about each man and identify his life and actions with his name.

Memorizing is learning the list. Meditating is focusing on the man and his heart, getting to know his virtues. Likewise, memorizing Scripture puts the living Word of God in your mind.

Meditating on the verse involves your entire being. Your spirit is activated and responds to the Word of God. You may not realize what is happening, but when you meditate on God's Word, the healing power of the Word of God is activated. "For they (My words) are life to those who find them, and health to all their flesh." (Proverbs 4:22)

Meditating causes God's Word to drop 18 inches from our minds into our hearts – into the very center of our being. God places a very high priority on what is in our hearts. He knows exactly what we believe deep down inside our hearts. "...God knoweth your hearts..." (Luke 16:15 KJV)

This is where the Holy Spirit lives. When we get God's Word into our hearts, it goes into storage. It is there just waiting to be used. When a problem comes up in our lives and we need a specific verse of Scripture, the Holy Spirit will bring it to our minds. Jesus said, "...And He will cause you to recall (will remind you of, bring to your remembrance) everything I have told you." (John 14:26 AMP)

The key to life is the Word of God! Our Father instructs us to fill our hearts with Scripture. "Let the word of God dwell in you richly, in all wisdom, teaching and admonishing one another in psalms and hymns and spiritual songs, singing with grace in your heart to the Lord." (Colossians 3:16)

Our hearts will store as many verses of Scripture as we can put in them. When we receive a negative or depressing thought, we can immediately refute it with a verse that we know. We understand how computers store data. We have verses stored for us to retrieve to use as weapons. We program our hearts with truths of the Word of God. "How blessed is the man whose strength is in Thee; in whose heart are the highways to Zion!" (Psalm 84:5, NAS).

The more we fill our hearts with God's Word, the more we'll rejoice because when our hearts are filled with the pure truth of God's Word, we will have great spiritual insight when we need it. "The precepts of the Lord are right, rejoicing the heart; the commandment of the Lord is pure and bright, enlightening the eyes..." (Psalm 19:8, AMP).

The more we meditate on God's Word, the more it will come alive to us. With each passing week, the Holy Spirit will unveil more and more of God's magnificent truth to us. Our hearts will be in awe of the magnificent spiritual truth of God's Word. "...my heart stands in awe of Your words..." (Psalm 119:161, AMP).

As we meditate more and more on the verses of Scripture that we have selected, we will realize that they are *much more* than just a few words on a small card. These words will come alive! We will realize that these verses of Scripture actually reveal the living God – the Creator of the entire universe – speaking directly to us, personalizing His instructions to us, showing us exactly how to use them in our lives.

Many people try to stockpile money and possessions for security in a time of emergency. We instinctively understand the need to "store up," but God does not want us to hoard material things. In fact, His Word specifically warns us. *He instructs us to store up His Word.* If we store up God's Word in our hearts, our spiritual ears will be open to His wisdom and we'll understand His plan for our lives. "...accept my words and store up my commands within you, turning your ear to wisdom and applying your heart to understanding..." (Proverbs 2:1-2 NIV)

There is no greater security on the face of this earth than a heart that is filled to overflowing with the Word of God. Our Father instructs us to work diligently at the process of meditating on His Word so that these verses of Scripture will remain in our hearts for the rest of our lives, always being available to us. "...Let thine heart retain my words..." (Proverbs 4:4 KJV)

Every aspect of our lives should revolve around His Word living in our hearts. "...lay up these My words in your [mind and] heart and in your [entire] being..." (Deuteronomy 11:18 AMP)

Our Father instructs us to write His Word down and then to keep it deep within our hearts. "...Guard my words as your most precious possession. Write them down, and also keep them deep within your heart." (Proverbs 7:2-3 TLB)

God's Word has a home – a place where it is meant to be – and that place is in the very center of our hearts. "Let the word [spoken by] the Christ, the Messiah, have its home (in your hearts and minds) and dwell in you in [all its] richness..." (Colossians 3:16 AMP)

The key to our lives here on earth is for God's Word, revealed by the Holy Spirit, to be our life's reference for all our words, thoughts and actions. When we grasp the tremendous significance of this truth, we'll realize the importance of meditating continually on God's Word. This should be a constant process, day and night, every day of our lives. "My son, attend to my words; consent and submit to my sayings. Let them not depart from your sight; keep them in the center of your heart" (Proverbs 4:20-21, AMP).

God's Word tells us that *wisdom is the principal thing.* "Therefore, get wisdom. And in all your getting, get understanding." (Proverbs 4:7) "My son, if your heart is wise, My own heart also will be glad ..." (Proverbs 23:15 NAS)

Some people think that Bible study is dry. They are wrong. Nothing is more exciting than to have God's Word continually flowing into our hearts! When this happens, we come alive spiritually. We understand great truths that were hidden in the past. If we continually fill our hearts with the Word of God, we will be guided to a long, full, successful life. "...keep my commands in your heart, for they will prolong your life many years and bring you prosperity." (Proverbs 3:1-2, NIV)

"If you live in Me [abide vitally united to Me] and My words remain in you and continue to live in your hearts, ask whatever you will, and it shall be done for you." (John 15:7 AMP). Abide is a word to study. Abiding in God and dwelling in God are two instructions God has given us.

The more we meditate on God's Word, the more firmly it will become established in our hearts. Our faith in God will be extremely solid. Nothing will shake us. No matter what comes at us, we won't be afraid. Our faith in God will be so strong that fear won't be able to get a foothold. Our faith in God through Christ Jesus will cause us to be triumphant. "He will have no fear of bad news; his heart is steadfast, trusting in the Lord. His heart is secure, he will have no fear; in the end he will look in triumph on his foes." (Psalm 112:7-8 NIV)

Success is living in the will of God for our lives. (See our book, *God's Plan for Your Life*) With God's Word as our compass, we will not be dampened or deterred by anything. "The law of his God is in his heart; none of his steps shall slide." (Psalm 37:31 KJV)

How sad we are for anyone who goes to church and does not walk closely with the Risen Savior. We weep for such a person. To sing songs of worship and hymns and not have a close relationship with the One who lived a perfect life and died, so that we would be redeemed would be tragic indeed. Whoever goes to church regularly and sings and praises the Lord, but whose heart is not filled with God's Word is missing so much of what is available. Living in God's Word brings you close to our heavenly Father Who loves us each so much. "These people honor me with their lips, but their hearts are far from me." (Matthew 15:8, NIV)

Heaven, indeed, for us begins the moment we believe. We enter the kingdom of heaven, even though we are still residents of earth. "I write these things to you who believe in the name of the Son of God, so that you may know that you have eternal life." (I John 5:13) Our deep joy in knowing our heavenly Father through His Son, Jesus Christ is the reality that from the moment we first believe and receive Christ Jesus as our Lord and Savior, we know that we have entered eternal life. We have the honor and privilege of living in God's presence every minute of every hour of every day while we are still on earth. "Go therefore and make disciples of all nations, baptizing them in the name of the Father, of the Son, and of the Holy Spirit, teaching them to observe all that I have commanded you. And behold, I am with you always, to the end of the age." (Matthew 28: 19-20) When we pass from this life to the next, we will change residences. Heaven will be our home. (John 5:24)

In case you missed it! Here's what you must do now! Go to https://lamplight.net and for free listen to or download Jack himself talking directly to you about why and how to Study the Bible. I guarantee you'll be blessed!

CHAPTER SEVEN

From Our Hearts to Our Mouths

L et's look now at a subject that isn't usually connected with studying the *Bible*-continually speaking God's Word with our mouths. As we will soon see, God's Word clearly shows us that speaking God's Word is essential if our *Bible* study is to have practical application in our lives.

Jack, 1985: As a *Bible* teacher and Christian counselor for the past ten years, I have seen many Christians attend church regularly and study the *Bible* faithfully and still not walk victoriously. Many sincere, devoted, caring Christians fail to live victorious lives because of a lack of understanding of the facts that will be brought out in this chapter.

If we don't fill our minds with God's Word and speak it every day, we may speak words that do not honor God. "If anyone considers himself religions and yet does not keep a tight rein on his tongue, he deceives himself and his religion is worthless." (James 1:26, NIV) The tongue reflects what is in the mind.

We know the principle of sowing and reaping. We reap what we sow. God's Word is alive and powerful. (Hebrews 4:12) Know that speaking God's Word is one of the most life-changing weapons you have. "So shall My word be that goes forth from My mouth; It shall not return to Me void, But it shall accomplish what I please, And it shall prosper in the thing for which I sent it:" (Isaiah 55:11) "From the fruit of a man's mouth he enjoys good..." (Proverbs 13:2 NAS) Plan to speak God's Word every day as you read it and meditate upon it. Be certain to speak it aloud, knowing that you are implementing a tool that will bring good.

Unfortunately, this subject of speaking the Word of God is very controversial. The controversy has been caused by the misuse of speaking God's Word with selfish motives, as if God were an online store with one-day delivery. This teaching is false teaching and selfish teaching. "...the kingdom of God consists of and is based on not talk but power (moral power and excellence of soul)." (I Corinthians 4:20 AMP)

A delightful article by Matt Slick states that he heard from a professor, "There is a God and you are not Him!" (See https://carm.org) I can think of a few prayers that I prayed in past years, fervently, and now how very thankful I am that God did not answer those prayers. Our job is not to dictate to God our will, but to spend our days so immersing ourselves into the heart of God that God's will becomes our will.

Speaking God's Word daily is a key to dwelling in God and God dwelling in us. "Now, therefore, you are no longer strangers and foreigners, but fellow citizens with the saints and members of the household of God, having been built on the foundation of the apostles and prophets, Jesus Christ Himself being the chief cornerstone, in whom the whole building, being fitted together, grows into a holy temple in the Lord, in whom you also are being built together for a dwelling place of God in the Spirit." (Ephesians 2:19-22)

We have to fill our hearts with God's Word before its power can be released through our mouths. "The heart of the wise teacheth his mouth, and addeth learning to his lips." (Proverbs 16:23, KJV).

'But what does it say? "The word is near you, in your mouth and in your heart" (that is, the word of faith which we preach): that if you confess with your mouth the Lord Jesus and believe in your heart that God raised Him from the dead, you will be saved. For with the heart one believes unto righteousness, and with the mouth confession is made unto salvation."' (Romans 10:8-10)

On three different occasions, these verses point out the connection that God makes between our hearts and our mouths. These verses of Scripture are the foundation for our salvation. Before we can be reborn spiritually, we must believe in our hearts and confess with our mouths that Jesus Christ is our Savior. *This same principle that starts our lives as Christians must be applied throughout our lives, so that we live in the glorious victory of Jesus Christ.*

If we believe God's Word and don't continually activate its power with our mouths, we are like a person with a high-powered car in the driveway with a key in the ignition, but never turning the key to start the car. Begin a daily habit of speaking God's Word. Speak it every time you read or meditate upon the *Bible.* Carry *Bible* verses with you. Carry the following verses with you and rotate them, praying them to our Father as you speak them:

"But if they had stood in My counsel, And had caused My people to hear My words, Then they would have turned them from their evil way And from the evil of their doings." (Jeremiah 23:22 NKJV)

"For I am not ashamed of the gospel of Christ, for it is the power of God to salvation for everyone who believes, for the Jew first and also for the Greek." (Romans 1:16 NKJV)

"In the beginning was the Word, and the Word was with God, and the Word was God." (John 1:1 NKJV)

"And the Word became flesh and dwelt among us, and we beheld His glory, the glory as of the only begotten of the Father, full of grace and truth." (John 1:14 NKJV)

"How then shall they call on Him in whom they have not believed? And how shall they believe in Him of whom they have not heard? And how shall they hear without a preacher?" (Romans 10:14 NKJV)

Your commission from God is to speak His Word to others after you have received Him into your heart through His Son Jesus Christ. Commit the following verse to your heart, so you will always be ready to speak of the joy that is within you to others. "But sanctify the Lord God in your hearts, and always be ready to give a defense to anyone who asks you a reason for the hope that is within you, with meekness and fear." (I Peter 3:15 NJKV) So, the following verses tucked into your heart will give the answer!

"Sirs, what must I do to be saved? So they said, "Believe on the Lord Jesus Christ, and you will be saved, you and your household." (Acts 16:30b, 31 NKJV)

"For all have sinned and fall short of the glory of God." (Romans 3:23 NKJV)

"For the wages of sin is death, but the gift of God is eternal life in Christ Jesus our Lord," (Romans 6:23 NKJV)

"For by grace you have been saved through faith, and that not of yourselves; it is the gift of God, not of works, lest anyone should boast." (Ephesians 2:8-9 NKJV)

"For He made Him who knew no sin to be sin for us, that we might become the righteousness of God in Him." (II Corinthians 5:21 NKJV)

"For the wages of sin is death, but the gift of life is eternal life in Christ Jesus our Lord." (Romans 6:23 NKJV)

"But as many as received Him, to them He gave the right to become children of God, to those who believe in His name:" (John 1:12 NKJV)

"These things have I written to you who believe in the name of the Son of God, that you may know that you have eternal life, and that you may continue to believe in the name of the Son of God." (I John 5:13 NKJV)

These life-giving verses provide the magnificent gift of eternal life to everyone who would come and receive it. Write each verse on a three by five card. Go over them every day until you know them. They will be written on your heart. When you speak to someone, you don't have to give the chapter and verse. Just give the glorious message of salvation in Christ Jesus to everyone you meet. The Holy Spirit will direct you.

You do not need to present all these verses each time you share Jesus Christ with someone, but they are of great value to know in your heart.

Why the urgency to speak of Christ Jesus and eternal life to everyone you meet, especially your family?

'And Jesus answered and said to them: Take heed that no one deceives you. For many will come in My name, saying, "I am the Christ," and will deceive many. And you will hear of wars and rumors of wars. See that you are not troubled; for all these things must come to pass, but the end is not yet. For nation will rise up against nation, and kingdom against kingdom. And there will be famines, pestilences, and earthquakes in various places. All these are the beginning of sorrows.

'Then they will deliver you up to tribulation and kill you, and you will be hated by all nations for My name's sake. And then many will be offended, will betray one another, and will hate one another. Then many false prophets will rise up and deceive many. And because lawlessness will abound, the love of many will grow cold. But he who endures to the end shall be saved. And this gospel of the kingdom will be preached in all the world as a witness to all nations, and then the end will come.' (Matthew 24:4-14 NKJV) Dear friends, you have a part to play in these last days.

As you can see, we are living in the times described. "For the Lord Himself will descend from heaven with a shout, with the voice of an archangel, and with the trumpet of God. And the dead in Christ will rise first. Then we who are alive and remain shall be caught up together with them in the clouds to meet the Lord in the air. And thus we shall always be with the Lord."

(I Thessalonians 4:16-17 NKJV)

The Holy Spirit will empower you and give you the courage to speak to everyone you meet. I pray right now that the Holy Spirit will touch you and ignite you to just naturally speak of Jesus Christ to everyone you meet, in the name of Jesus I pray. Amen. Please let me know when you experience a freedom to speak to others about Jesus Christ. I consider it to be one of the greatest treasures in my life.

To speak easily of Jesus Christ, you must have the Word of God immersed in your heart. Jesus explained this when He said, "...out of the abundance of the heart the mouth speaketh." (Matthew 12:34, KJV) Jesus is explaining that whatever you put into your mind and your heart will come out of your mouth. You will speak what you have entered into your mind or heart. Plant the verses explaining the magnificent gift of God, salvation bringing glory to this life and life eternal with Jesus Christ.

When we are in a crisis, *whatever our hearts are filled with* – positive or negative – *will* pour out of our mouths. If our hearts are filled with something and we believe deeply in it, we *cannot stop it* from coming out of our mouths even if we try. "...the human tongue can be tamed by no man..." (James 3:8, AMP).

In other words, we *cannot* control our tongues with willpower. In a crisis, sooner or later we'll blurt out what we really believe. The key to our tongues is what we really believe in our hearts. The secret to releasing what we believe in our hearts is to fill them abundantly with the Word of God. Our mouths will speak what our heart believes.

Again, and again, this principle is taught in God's Word. Jesus said, "...those things which proceed out of the mouth come forth from the heart..." (Matthew 15:18, KJV).

Take a careful look at the following well-known words from Jesus Christ. "For verily I say unto you, That whosoever shall say unto this mountain, Be thou removed, and be thou cast into the sea; and shall not doubt in his heart, but shall believe that those things which he saith shall come to pass; he shall have whatsoever he saith." (Mark 11:23, KJV)

Whenever we are faced with a "mountain" – any difficult problem that must be overcome – Jesus tells us open our mouths and speak to that problem by releasing the spiritual power of God's Word. Soon we will have a history of God's faithfulness in our lives. Keep a record of what God does in your life and your family's lives. You will comprehend that God's Word is a part of the armor of God.

Add Ephesians 6:10-18 to your artillery of verses committed to your heart. Learn the whole armor of God and exercise at the same time! Go to https://youtube.com and put in "Praise Moves-The 91st Psalm." You will do praise moves (stretching exercises) while you commit the verses to your heart. "...he who has My word, let him speak My word faithfully..." (Jeremiah 23:28, AMP).

Watch and see how God will empower you each day to speak what you have committed to your heart. Before you pounce out of bed each morning, ask your heavenly Father for opportunities to share Jesus Christ and the Word of God with everyone you meet that day. Keep a record in your daily planner of each encounter. You will be so excited to read back over what God has accomplished through you. "The mouth of the righteous [those harmonious with God] brings forth skillful and godly Wisdom..." (Proverbs 10:31 AMP)

In the natural world, power is released physically and financially. *In the spiritual realm, one way power is released is by the words we speak.* The Word of God is full of spiritual power. "...no word from God shall be without power or impossible of fulfillment." (Luke 1:37, AMP)

God's Word is supernaturally alive. Negative words also have power. "The tongue has the power of life and death ..." (Proverbs 18:21 NIV). You can find on the Internet reports of many experiments with plants. An Example is that one plant is spoken over with kind words, another plant is spoken over with negative words, and another plant is not spoken over at all. The results are that the plant spoken over with kind words thrives the best of all the plants. If plants respond to both kind and negative words, just think of what kind words and unkind words to do humans. If you fill your mind and heart with the Word of God, you will be much less likely to ever hurt someone with unkind words. You will bless everyone with kind words, even better with the Word of God.

God's Word is spiritually alive. Words of worry, fear and doubt are spiritually dead.

No matter how bad a crisis might seem, refuse to waver. Keep on speaking God's Word. "...the speech of the upright rescues them." (Proverbs 12:6, NIV)

No matter what subject we decide to study in the *Bible*, we must plant the Scripture pertaining to it into our hearts and speak it out of our mouths. God gave us a clear example in the first chapter of the *Bible*. See how many times it reads "*God says*" and you will see the power of the spoken Word of God. If we study the four gospels carefully, we will see how Jesus spoke each of His miracles. The power of God's Word is amazing. "How forcible are right words! ..." (Job 6:25, KJV)

Our mouths are like fountains. If our hearts are filled with the Word of God, spiritual power will flow out of those fountains. "The mouth of the righteous is a fountain of life..." (Proverbs 10:11, NIV)

Our words are seeds. Plant glorious seeds of the Word of God every day. "From the fruit of his lips a man is filled with good things..." (Proverbs 12:14, NIV)

"The lips of the [uncompromisingly] righteous know [and therefore utter] what is acceptable..." (Proverbs 10:32 AMP)

We could spend a lot of time on the phrase "uncompromisingly righteous." How very much we desire to honor God every moment. Writing His Word on our hearts is a key to being "uncompromisingly righteous."

When we continually speak God's Word, we are built up and strengthened. We also build up and strengthen others. "Let no unwholesome word proceed from your mouth, but only such a word as is good for edification according to the need of the moment, that it may give grace to those who hear." (Ephesians 4:29 NAS) Before you speak, test your thoughts to see if they are filled with the grace of God.

This is why God's Word says, "...faith cometh by hearing, and hearing by the word of God." (Romans 10:17 KJV). I cannot emphasize enough the importance of committing the salvation verses to your heart. Carry them with you and go over them again and again until speaking them is as easy as breathing. "And how shall they preach unless they are sent? As it is written: How beautiful are the feet of those who preach the gospel of peace, Who bring glad tidings of good things!" (Romans 10:15 NKJV).

We need to have such an abundance of God's Word in our hearts that it will overflow continually out of our mouths. We must realize that faith grows from the *spoken* word of God ("rhema") and *not* from the *written* word of God ("logos"). Study and meditate continually in God's Word in order to put the "logos" into your mind and your heart. Then "rhema" will flow out of your mouth.

Faith comes from hearing the Word of God. Faith *will* grow from continually hearing *others* speak the Word of God, but I have found that *faith grows much more rapidly when our ears continually hear our lips speaking the Word of God!* When our hearts are full of God's Word and our mouths speak it continually, a supernatural effect takes place in our spirits.

I don't let a day go by without opening my mouth several times to speak the Word of God. If we get into the habit of continuously filling our hearts with the truth of God's Word, and then speaking this powerful truth with our mouths, our lives will be transformed! When our ears continually hear our mouths speak the same words that God says, our faith will grow tremendously.

CHAPTER EIGHT

---◆◆◆◆---

Judy's Bible Study Methods

The subject method of studying the *Bible* is extremely valuable for finding answers to life's issues. God has a plan that is unfolding. We must know God's plan, His history, His plans for the present, and for the future. The *Bible* is the history of the world. We must know that history. As we saw, according to descriptions of the last days before we meet Jesus Christ in the air, we are living in the time described. "For the Lord Himself will descend from heaven and with a shout, with the voice of an archangel, and with the trumpet of God. And the dead in Christ will rise first. Then we who are alive and remain shall be caught up together with them in the clouds to meet the Lord in the air. And thus we shall always be with the Lord. Therefore comfort one another with these words." (I Thessalonians 4:15-1 NKJV)

Can you see how important knowing God's Word, the *Bible* is? We recommend the *New King James Version* for accuracy and ease of understanding. My daughter gave me a *The One Year Bible* in the New Living Translation for Christmas in 2013. I have been enjoying it each year.

Sometimes I write in a notebook a short summary of what I read each day. Sometimes I choose a few verses to put on three by five cards to learn. I keep a list of topics each year that I want to focus upon and look for verses on that topic. I began this method when I was in high school.

This is Jack's topical method. It is wonderful to do when you are reading through the *Bible.*

Each day as you read through the *Bible,* look for interesting history that you can share with others in daily conversation. Write in a notebook the history that you want to remember and share with others. God instructs us to speak the Word of God all day long. "And these words which I command you today shall be in your heart. You shall teach them diligently to your children, and shall talk of them when you sit in your house, when you walk by the way, when you lie down, and when you rise up. You shall bind them as a sign on your hand and they shall be as frontlets between your eyes." (Deuteronomy 6:6-8) This verse definitely can be applied to the entire *Bible.*

Sometimes I look to see where I am in my read-through-the-*Bible* book and listen to it on the audio *Bible* on https://biblegateway.com. Sometimes I listen to a book over and over again, especially Philippians, as we were going through it at my church, Christ Point Church in Concord, North Carolina. My pastor, Pastor James Metzger, brought out background and details that made the study so alive. Enjoy Pastor James in the book of Philippians at https://christpoint.com. Click on Media and then click on The Letter to the Philippians. You will be transformed by your journey through the book of Philippians, the book of joy.

I always choose a church that focuses on studying the *Bible* book by book. My church in Palm Harbor, Florida, Calvary Chapel Palm Harbor, was devoted to studying the *Bible* book by book. Pastor Brett Robinson has a study of the book of Revelation that is absolutely life changing. I emphatically recommend that you go to https://ccpalmharbor.org, click on Media, then on the Sermons page, then on Revelation. You will go on a journey that will change your life!

Read and study the Word of God on *Bible* applications, such as the You Version. Go to https://youversion.com or https://mybible.com. You will find *Bible* reading plans, many devotions, videos of books of the *Bible*, including the gospels of Matthew, Mark, Luke, and John. Download an application to your cell phone or download it to any device that you choose. Keep the Word of God with you wherever you go.

Reading through a chapter of Proverbs each day will impart to each family member what happens when you make right choices and what happens when you make wrong choices. Even when children are very young, read a chapter of Proverbs aloud each day. Begin writing the Word of God on your children's hearts. Later in life, when a temptation arises, your family member will have Proverbs written on his or her heart and remember the consequences of making the wrong choice.

Read Proverbs Chapter One on the first day of the month. Read Proverbs Chapter Two on the second day of each month and continue throughout the month, reading the Proverbs chapter for that day. Ask each child which verse stood out. Discuss each of these chosen verses as a family. Select one verse for each family member to write on a three by five card to carry and consider all day long. Each family member can act out his or her chosen verse, exaggerating the positive and the negative of each verse. The family will laugh together hilariously. The book of

Proverbs was given to us to warn us of the dangers of certain choices. We are also told the rewards of certain choices. Each family member will be reminded each day that God's Word is filled with wisdom and that wisdom leads to living the best life possible to live on earth.

God has provided the Psalms as expressions of the deepest emotions. If you read five Psalms each day, you will have read through the whole book of Psalms in one month. Read Psalms 1, 31, 61, 91, and 121 on the first day of the month. On the second day of the month, read Psalm 2, 32, 62, 92, and 122. Continue to read the next five Psalms throughout the month. You will find that if you read each Psalm with expression that you will experience emotions, such as extreme sorrow, extreme anger, extreme disappointment, and extreme joy. I think the Psalms provide exercise for our emotions in a very healthy way. Enjoy each Psalm to the fullest. Pray each Psalm to your heavenly Father.

Psalm 119 takes longer, so adjust for it. Enjoy Psalm 119 as the book that describes all the benefits of writing the Word of God on your heart. Write Psalm 100, Psalm 100, Psalm 91, and Psalm 139 on your heart as well as all the Psalms that speak to you in a magnificent way. Sing the Psalms. If places and events in the *Bible* are mentioned in a Psalm, look up the names given to enlarge your understanding of the Psalm.

There is much evidence in the *Bible* showing that its complexity was inspired by God. One evidence is the use of acrostics. An acrostic is a poem or other form of writing in which the first letter (or syllable or word) of each line (or paragraph or other recurring feature in the text) spells out a word, message, or the alphabet.

Psalm 119 is one of the acrostic Psalms in the *Bible*. Its 176 verses are divided into 22 stanzas, one for each of the characters that make up the Hebrew alphabet. Unlike other acrostics that contain only one verse for each of the 22 Hebrew letters, Psalm 119 contains eight verses for each letter, totaling 176 verses. The 22 stanzas each contain eight verses starting with the same Hebrew letter. The Word of God is the topic of Psalm 119 and is contained in every verse, except verses 84, 121, and 122. The purpose of an acrostic Psalm is to present a complete picture of that Psalm's message. All translations of the *Bible* should reveal to the reader that both the content and the structure of the *Bible* were inspired by God.

I want to include in the description of my *Bible* study methods, one of the reasons I study the *Bible*. The last instructions that Jesus gave to His disciples after his resurrection but before He returned to heaven were:

'And Jesus came and spoke to them, saying, "All authority has been given to Me in heaven and on earth. Go therefore and make disciples of all the nations, baptizing them in the name of the Father and of the Son and of the Holy Spirit, teaching them to observe all things that I have commanded you; and lo, I am with you always, even to the end of the age. Amen."' (Matthew 28:18-20)

As we have mentioned previously, how can people know the message of salvation in Christ Jesus unless someone tells them. When Jesus said, "Go therefore and make disciples of all nations, He was speaking to His disciples. When you choose to be a follower of Jesus Christ, you become His disciple. These instructions are for you. They are for every disciple of Jesus Christ.

I pray right now in the name of Jesus Christ that the Holy Spirit Who lives inside of you will empower you to speak of Jesus to everyone you meet. Amen. The urgency of letting people know what awaits them when they choose to follow Jesus Christ must overrule your shyness. Your shyness is yourself speaking. Tell yourself that you have important kingdom business to complete and for yourself to get out of the way!

Once you begin to speak of Jesus, your shyness will melt away. Each day when someone asks you how you are, you can reply, "I'm blessed in the Lord Jesus Christ and I pray His blessing upon you," looking at the person directly into his or her eyes. No one has ever acted offended when I have greeted him or her this way. Most people say, "Thank you" and sometimes, "I pray the same for you."

Write the salvation verses on three by five cards. Practice sharing Christ with a family member or a friend. Take turns being the person sharing Christ and the person receiving Christ.

When I am at the grocery store and am asked if I would like help taking my groceries to my car, I always answer

"Yes." Then I have time to ask the person, usually a student, what he or she is studying and what his or her interests are. Then after I have established a relationship, I ask if the person has come to know the Lord Jesus Christ. If the person does not know our Lord, I know that I do not have much time. I do not want to deter the person from working, so I have to speak quickly and briefly. So, I ask if the person has a *Bible*. Then I say coming to know the Lord Jesus Christ means that you confess your sins and ask Him to come into your heart. I ask the person if he or she would like to do that right now. If not, I say that in the quietness of your heart, you can ask Jesus Christ to be Lord of your life. Then I say that telling someone is important. All this is happening while we are unloading the groceries. It is comfortable and natural. I proceed only as the person is open to hearing.

If a person is not open for me to proceed, I say that Jesus Christ loves him or her very much and if the day comes that you want to know Him, here is how you do it. Then I quickly say that you confess your sins and ask Him into your heart to be Lord of your life and then tell someone what you did. I have not offended the person at all.

One of my favorite places to share Jesus Christ is on an airplane. I usually select the unwanted middle seat. This way I have two opportunities to share Christ. I wait for the Holy Spirit to open the way to speak. Sometimes we are almost ready to land and the way is clear to speak. This might be when a person has chosen to sleep during the entire flight. I pray for an opportunity to speak to the person. You would be surprised how much can be said during the time the plane is landing and while we are waiting to get off the plane. Sometimes I am between two Christians and we have a glorious time together for the whole flight. Sometimes one is quite open to hear and the other is not. So, at the last minute I speak a blessing over the one who is not open to hear and the blessing is always received with a smile and a word of thanks.

Another application of the Word of God is to give to the poor. "He who has pity on the poor lends to the Lord, and He will pay back what he has given." (Proverbs 19:17 NKJV) If you have ever been poor, you easily give to the poor. You remember. If you have never been poor, you give to the poor out of obedience to God's instructions. I was talking to my oldest son, Brad, today, and he reminded me of the Christmas and the candy bars. That was the Christmas where we went into a grocery store and I told the children they could have any candy bar in the store. That was their Christmas. Brad reminded me that I did not even like for them to eat candy bars, which made the gesture even more meaningful. So, I remember.

Paul said that he knew what lack was and he knew what plenty was and he would be content in whatever situation he would find himself. "I know how to be abased, and I know how to abound. Everywhere and in all things, I have learned both to be full and to be hungry, both to abound and to suffer need." (Philippians 4:12 NKJV) Plan to bless the poor with food and with clothing and with whatever else you have to give. "Do not withhold good from those to whom it is due When it is in the power of your hand to do so." (Proverbs 3:27)

One of my favorite websites is Every Home for Christ (https://www.ehc.org), founded by Dick Eastman in 1946 and is dedicated to reaching every home in the world with the gospel of Jesus Christ. Prayer is the key to evangelism and discipleship. All three areas make up the core of Every Home for Christ. Last year 118 million homes were reached with the gospel of Jesus Christ. Spend time on the website.

You will find free prayer maps for the world and for the United States. You will find the names of the Supreme Court justices, so you can pray for them. You can download a free book telling of many of the remarkable life transformations that have occurred through Every Home for Christ. There are offices in 150 countries with local people ministering to their neighbors and countrymen in their own language. You will find videos, prayer for America, and so much more. In the last five years, over 400 million homes have been personally reached with the gospel and Jesus Christ and followed up with over 70 million who have responded to the gospel. To know what God is doing today around the world, spend time on this website. You will be so encouraged. Participate in any way that you can.

I so enjoy praying for the one or two states listed for each day of the month and for the five or six countries listed for the day for prayer. The population of each state or country is provided as well as the percent of Christians in the state or country. The president of each country is provided for prayer. There are five verses that I have learned because of praying them so many times. They cover the areas of praying for open hands to minister the gospel (Proverbs 3:27); open doors to spread the gospel (Colossians 4:23); open minds to receive the gospel (Acts 26:17); open hearts to embrace the gospel (II Corinthians 4:6); and open heavens that the Gospel will transform nations (Isaiah 45:8). I enjoy the free book, *A Watchman's Guide to Praying God's Promises* (free to download).

Download *Look What God is Doing!* as well, to see what God is doing throughout the world through Every Home for Christ. Participate in the online School of Prayer.

Currently 342,012 homes are reached each day with a total of two billion already reached. Currently 53,422 people respond to the gospel each day with a total of 211 million people responding to the gospel. Currently, 73 Christ groups are formed each day with a total of 239, 649. Spend time on the website, www.ehc.org and see what God can do through you!

Another way to see what God is doing in the world today is to visit Uncharted Ministries' website, https://unchartedministries.com. Tom and Jo Ann Doyle have been ministering in the Middle East since 2001.

I have purchased all of Tom's books. I gave the book, *The Incredible Journey,* by Tom Doyle, an amazing summary of each book of the *Bible,* to 32 people as Christmas gifts. I also have given the other books as gifts as well. The books reveal the true stories of what has happened to those who receive Christ in nations in the Middle East where persecution is extremely high. Reading the true accounts, written by those who experienced them, is mandatory. Every believer in Christ Jesus must know what is happening to our brothers and sisters in nations where persecution is extreme. When you become aware of what is happening today, you will never be the same. Your prayer life will change. The giving of your income will change. You will receive the call to help in any way you can.

For daily prayer go to https://liveprayer.com Our friend, Bill Keller, founded *liveprayer* as the first live prayer website online. He now ministers to over two and a half million people daily. Retired pastors answer the prayer requests every day. You can receive a daily prayer in your email box. The purpose of liveprayer.com is to have a place where you can go day or night to pray. At 11 pm to 12 am Monday through Friday, you can watch *liveprayer* on the *liveprayer* Roku channel.

Just in case you missed it! What you need to do right now! Go to https://lamplight.net and for free listen to or download Jack Hartman, speaking to you in his legendary voice the powerful Word of God. Yes, you can just flat out have this priceless audio of Jack Hartman on How to Study the Bible for free!

CHAPTER NINE

———◆◆◆●———

The Final Step – Obeying God's Instructions

Would it make any sense for someone to go through medical school, become an M.D. and never practice medicine? Would it make any sense for someone to go through college, study architecture, become an architect and never design a building? Does it make any sense to study the *Bible*, learn exactly what it says to do and *not obey its instructions*?

Any book that tells us how to study the *Bible* also should tell us how important it is to *do* what the Word of God tells us to do. In this book, we have discussed how to study and meditate on God's Word, how to fill our hearts with it and speak it with our mouths. What is the purpose of all this effort? "…the word is very near you, in your mouth and in your mind and in your heart, so that you can do it." (Deuteronomy 30:14 AMP)

The reason for getting God's Word in our minds, in our hearts and in our mouths is so we will *do what it says to do*!

Let's look again at Joshua 1:8, the verse of Scripture that tells us how to be successful in everything we do. We have already looked at this verse of Scripture for its instructions to meditate in God's Word day and night and to speak it continually. We do these two things so that we can carefully do everything that God's Word tells us to do. "This book of the law shall not depart from your mouth, but you shall meditate on it day and night, so that you may be careful to do according to all that is written in it; for then you will make your way prosperous, and then you will have success." (Joshua 1:8, NAS) One definition of "successful and prosperous" is to have everything you need to carry out God's plan for your life at the exact right time.

"Keep the charge of the Lord your God, to walk in His ways, to keep His statutes, His commandments, His ordinances, and His testimonies, according to what is written in the Law of Moses, that you may succeed in all that you do and wherever you turn." (I Kings 2:3 NAS) People who lived before the time of the resurrection of Jesus did not have Jesus living inside of them. They had to do their best to obey God's commandments.

We live in the time after the resurrection of Jesus and His ascension to heaven. Now He's sitting at the right hand of God. "But God, who is rich in mercy, because of His great love with which He loved us, even when we were dead in trespasses, made us alive together with Christ (by grace you have been saved), and raised us up together, and made us sit together in the heavenly places in Christ Jesus, that in the ages to come He might show the exceeding riches of His grace in His kindness toward us in Christ Jesus." Ephesians 2:4-7 NKJV)

You are alive in Christ Jesus. You can do all things through Christ Jesus Who strengthens you. (Philippians 4:13) Understand clearly that you are not to live "trying" to please God and honor Him. You are to live in the power of the resurrection of Jesus Christ. Life is not "trying!" Life is living in the presence of Almighty God all the time! If you are in Christ, and I believe that you are, you are sitting with Jesus Christ in heavenly places. You are not a citizen of the earth. You are a citizen of heaven already! "For our citizenship is in heaven, from which we also eagerly wait for the Savior, the Lord Jesus Christ." (Philippians 3:20)

The power of God resides within you. You have a choice each day. You can live on the mind level, the human effort level, or you can live in the power that resides inside of you, the resurrection power of Jesus Christ. "Now to Him who is able to do exceedingly abundantly above all that we ask or think, according to the power that works in us, to Him be glory in the church by Christ Jesus to all generations, forever and ever. Amen." (Ephesians 3:20-21) This verse, my friend, is one to write on your heart.

We become disciples of Jesus Christ by abiding in His Word, by saturating ourselves in it, studying and meditating on it continually. When we do, we'll learn God's instructions for our lives. The words "disciple" and "discipline" come from the same root. We must discipline ourselves to have a definite time and place to meet God in His Word every day.

If we abide in God's Word, we'll learn its great truths. Today some people believe there are not absolutes (except they are believing an absolute when they say there are no absolutes). These people think they find freedom in having no absolutes, freedom to do whatever they want whenever they want. "There is a way that seems right to a man, But its end is the way of death." (Proverbs 14:12)

You will find God's absolutes in His Word. They are absolute. "...If you abide in My word [hold fast to My teachings and live in accordance with them], you are truly

My disciples. And you will know the Truth, and the Truth will set you free." (John 8:31-32 AMP) If you desire freedom, surrender your life to Jesus Christ and abide in the Word of God.

One verse that warms my heart is: "I have no greater joy than to hear that my children walk in truth." (III John 4 KJV) Paul speaks of his children, those who have come to Christ and whom Paul has nurtured in their journey in Christ Jesus. Every Christian parent wants to experience this great joy. Jesus Christ abides in us. We abide in Him. "By this we know that we abide in Him, and He in us, because He has given us of His Spirit. And we have seen and testify that the Father has sent the Son as Savior of the world. Whoever confesses that Jesus is the Son of God, God abides in him, and he in God. And we have known and believed the love that God has for us. God is love, and he who abides in love abides in God, and God in him." (I John 4:13-16)

None of us will know what God's Word tells us to do unless we study and meditate continually in His Book of Instructions. Abiding in God will become automatic. Then our "computers" will be programmed with the Word of God, so that no matter what situation comes up, we will have the solution "programmed" into our hearts. As a result, we'll live in the will of God through His Word. "...if anyone keeps looking steadily into God's law for free men, he will not only remember it but he will do what it says, and God will greatly bless him in everything he does." (James 1:25 TLB)

In His magnificent Sermon on the Mount, Jesus placed great emphasis on *doing* what He tells us to do. He said that if we learn what God's Word says and then *do* it, our lives will be built on a solid, rock-like foundation and we will be able to stand up against any storms that come against us. However, if we hear the Word of God *without doing what it says*, our lives will be built on a foundation that is like sand and we'll crumble and fall apart when the storms of life come against us:

"… everyone who hears these words of mine and puts them into practice is like a wise man who built his house on the rock. The rain came down, the streams rose, and the winds blew and beat against that house; yet it did not fall, because it had its foundation on the rock. But everyone who hears these words of mine and does not put them into practice is like a foolish man who built his house on sand. The rain came down, the streams rose, and the winds blew and beat against that house, and it fell with a great crash." (Matthew 7:24-27 NIV).

Again, and again, we see that when the going gets tough, the keys to success are, (a) to *know* what God's Word says about that particular area and then, (b) to *do* what God's Word says to do. "…be doers of the Word [obey the message], and not merely listeners to it, betraying yourselves [into deception by reasoning contrary to the Truth]." (James 1:22 AMP).

The Amplified Bible explains this truth beautifully! We betray ourselves if we follow our human reasoning which may seem right to us, but actually does not line up with God's Word. God's ways are usually different from our ways. What seems logical to us is often different from what God instructs us to do. Therefore, understanding God's history, His plan to redeem us (buy us back), and His answers to every issue we will face is non-negotiable.

Jesus placed great emphasis on doing what He tells us to do. He pointed out that many of us say that He is our

Lord, go to church and think we lead good lives, but then don't do what He tells us to do. "...why call ye me, Lord, Lord, and do not the things which I say?" (Luke 6:46 KJV).

Can we say that Jesus is our Lord if we are not following His instructions? Then Jesus' mother and His brothers came along toward Him, but they could not get to Him because of the crowd. And it was told Him," Your mother and Your brothers are standing outside, desiring to have an interview with You." But He answered them, "My mother and My brothers are those who listen to the Word of God and do it!"' (Luke 8:19-21 AMP).

Suppose that a well-known person had written a book in an area where he was an acknowledged expert. Presume that each reader of this book had a problem in this area and asked for an appointment with this author. Suppose the author said he would only grant this appointment if each reader would guarantee that he had read the book and was doing his best to follow its instructions. If the reader wanted answers, he would first study the book to see if the answer is in the book. Then the reader could contact the author. Then the author would be willing to help the reader further.

God has written a book, the *Bible*. It contains every answer that any of us will ever need. We have spent years doing research for you. You can find answers in the *Bible* online by putting in your issue and adding —verse, or answer in the *Bible*." You can also go to our website, https://lamplight.net and see a chart of life issues or problems and which of our books is filled with the Word of God on that issue. We have completed 32 *Bible*-based books on specific topics, just for you.

Approach the *Bible* with reverent awe. Learn what it says to do and then follow these instructions.

"Blessed (happy, fortunate, to be envied) is everyone who fears, reveres, and worships the Lord, who walks in His ways and lives according to His commandments." (Psalm 128:1 AMP). Remember that you live in the time after the cross of Jesus Christ. You live with the power of God residing inside of you in Christ Jesus and the Holy Spirit. "For in Him we live and move and have our being …" (Acts 17:28). Abide in Christ Jesus.

"…blessed are those who hear the word of God and observe it." (Luke 11:28 NAS). Are you experiencing the joy of spending time with God in His Word? Watch the movie, The War Room, again if you have seen it or for the first time if you have not seen it. Then plan your special war room in your home, a place where you meet with God and both speak and listen. "…this is love for God: to keep his commands…" (I John 5:3 NIV).

Sometimes we pray for what God has already provided for us. We can know what God has provided for us by reading through His Word once each year. Every time we go through the *Bible*, we will have new eyes to see more that God has provided for us. "…it is your Father's good pleasure to give you the kingdom." (Luke 12:32 KJV).

Discover who walked with God in the *Bible*. Learn what is important to God. Learn what pleases God. "… No good thing will he withhold from those who walk along his paths." (Psalm 84:11 TLB).

God's love in Christ Jesus is the answer for the world today. Fear is rampant across the world. The love of God in Christ Jesus in and through you will make a difference in your world. "…whoever keeps His word, in him the love of God has truly been perfected ..." (I John 2:5 NAS). You can be the love of God to others.

Today fear is driving people to suicide. Fear is creating panic in so many lives. Financial unrest deceives people to commit fraud and steal. "There is no fear in love. But perfect love drives out fear, because fear has to do with punishment. The one who fears is not made perfect in love." (I John 4:18 NIV).

The more we obey our Father's instructions, the closer we will draw to Him. The closer we are to Him, the more His love will dominate our thoughts, emotions, words, and actions. The more His love permeates our lives, the less chance fear has of establishing a foothold.

To live without knowing the Word of God, the *Bible*, is like living without breath. The *Bible* is God-breathed. "All Scripture is given by inspiration of God, and is profitable for doctrine, for reproof, for correction, for instruction in righteousness, that the man of God may be complete, thoroughly equipped for every good work." (II Timothy 3:16-17).

Conclusion

O ur goal is to ignite in you a hunger to know God in Christ Jesus through His Word. We started with the different types of *Bibles* that you need and the aids you need for studying the *Bible*. We showed you how to meditate on the Word of God, how to get it from your mind into your heart and, from there, to speak it out of your mouth. We clarified the necessity of doing what God's Word says to do.

Our passion is for you to walk closely with your heavenly Father through His Son, Jesus Christ, our Lord, and to live in the resurrection power of Jesus Christ and of the Holy Spirit who resides inside of you. Our great joy will be for you to have a hunger to know our heavenly Father, His Son Jesus Christ, and the Holy Spirit through knowing the Word of God.

Our prayer is that you immerse yourself in God's Word, the *Bible*, each day at a specific place, at a specific time, with your study tools ready for you, and your *Bible* open and ready. We trust that you will choose to explore God's Word by the topical method and by reading through the *Bible* in a year as well as studying the *Bible* book by book. We trust that you will carry verses and passages with you every day and go over them as you have free moments, such as at a stoplight, on a coffee break, or between loads of wash. We desire that your mind and heart become so filled with God's Word that it pours out of your mouth like a river of living water to everyone you meet each day.

We perceive that God's wisdom will transform you into a person you never even dreamed that you could be. God's Word takes you to heights, depths, widths, and breadths that are beyond what you have ever experienced in your life. You never arrive at mastering God's Word. You spend your life swimming in the river of joy that God's Word brings. Your hunger for God's Word increases each day and is never quenched.

As you soar in the wisdom of God, you realize that you are becoming more like Jesus each day. You observe old traits that bothered you decreasing and soon they are gone. You see that what never bothered you previously now becomes a habit or action that you no longer want to include in your life. The closer you come to your heavenly Father, the more you desire to be like Him and let loose of anything that does not honor Him. You are learning to be in the "rest" of the Lord, that it is available as a permanent place to live, in the "rest" of God. You desire to stay there all the time. "There remains therefore a rest for the people of God. For he who has entered His rest has himself also ceased from his works as God did from His." (Hebrews 4:9-11 NKJV)

God has provided a rest for each of us that keeps us in His rest all the time. We no longer strive to complete God's will, but we rest in His power to work in us to

Conclusion

complete His will. We still have much to complete before He comes for us, but the way we live no longer creates stress. We keep our hearts in the heart of God and see the world through His eyes with His passion. "The steps of a good man are ordered by the Lord, and He delights in his way." (Psalm 37:23 NKJV) Notice that God delights in your way!

You have come to the place where you live to please your heavenly Father. You wake up each morning with praise on your lips and a song in your heart. You pray each day for God to bring people into your life who are hungry to know Him. You are ever ready with the message of eternal life, salvation through Christ Jesus, a gift you will bestow on everyone you meet. "How beautiful upon the mountains Are the feet of him who brings good news, Who proclaims peace, Who brings glad tidings of good things, Who proclaims salvation, Who says to Zion, Your God reigns!" (Isaiah 52:7 NKJV)

How excited I will be to hear from you. I want to hear about your new history! I want to hear the results of your wielding the two-edged sword. "For the word of God is living and powerful, and sharper than any two-edged sword, piercing even to the division of soul and spirit, and of joints and marrow, and is a discerner of the thoughts and intents of the heart." (Isaiah 52:7) You are mightily equipped to do great exploits for the kingdom of God in Christ Jesus.

Jack and Judy

———•✦•——

Study Questions

O ur goal is for you to use this book as an individual or a group study. In all our books, we provide review questions for each chapter. You can easily find the answers in the chapter. In your group, be certain that everyone is included. Give time for the more reserved people to give their opinions. As you go over each question with discussion, at the end, ask if anyone else has a thought. You can create a group situation in which everyone is comfortable and feels free to speak. Each person in the group has a gift, or contribution to give. Our prayer is that every person in the group feels a beautiful bond with the group. You are growing in Christ Jesus together. You are not in an intellectual study, but your intellect is very important. As you enter the Word of God into your spirit, your intellect increases.

Dear friends, when you come to faith in Christ Jesus, you do not leave your intellect at the door. No! You have the privilege of receiving more wisdom than any person on earth who does not know Christ Jesus. You have the mind of Christ Jesus. "These things we also speak, not in words which man's wisdom teaches but which the Holy Spirit teaches, comparing spiritual things with spiritual.

But the natural man does not receive the things of the Spirit of God, for they are foolishness to him; nor can he know them, because they are spiritually discerned. But he who is spiritual judges as things, yet he himself is rightly judged by no one. For who has known the mind of the Lord that he may instruct Him? But we have the mind of Christ." (I Corinthians 2:13-16)

Your mind is exercised by use. Jack said so often that he believed that anyone who is in the Word of God faithfully and meditates upon it daily will keep his or her mind sharp. As important as exercise is the exercise of your brain daily.

The Word of God is Jesus. "In the beginning was the Word, and the Word as with God, and the Word was God." (John 1:1) "And the Word became flesh and dwelt among us, and we beheld His glory, the glory as of the only begotten of the Father, full of grace and truth. (John 1:14) Every time you experience the Word of God, you are experiencing Jesus Christ.

Enjoy reviewing our book by discussing the following questions for each chapter.

Chapter One – *Every Word in the Bible Comes from God*

1. What was the one thing Jack's friend recommended that he do to get himself out of his mess? (John 3:16)

2. Whose inspiration wrote the *Bible* and what can the *Bible* do to equip us for life? (I Thessalonians 2:13; II Timothy 3:16-17)

3. What message is found in every book of the *Bible*. Give some examples.

4. Explain what God's Word has given us. (II Corinthians 7:11; Hebrews 4:12; II Peter 1:34)

5. Explain how God's Word is spiritual food. (Jeremiah 15:16; Matthew 4:4)

6. Explain how God's Word transfers you from the kingdom of darkness to the kingdom of light. (Psalm 119105; Psalm 119:130; Ephesians 5:8)

7. How is the *Bible* different from other books? (Isaiah 40:6-8; Jeremiah 23:29; Matthew 24:35; Romans 11:33; I Peter 1:25)

Chapter Two – *The Foundation for Understanding God's Word*

1. Who cannot see the light of the gospel of Jesus Christ? (II Corinthians 4:3-4)

2. Who did Jesus promise would come after He ascended to heaven? Who would come? (John 16:13)

3. Who knows the thoughts of God? (I Corinthians 2:11-13)

4. What is the significance of the Holy Spirit in our lives? (I Corinthians 2:11-15)

5. What is a great prayer to pray each day? (Psalm 119:18-19)

6. What part of you never grows old? (II Corinthians 4:16)

7. How is the *Bible* a weapon? (Psalm 17:4; I John 5:18)

Chapter Three – *Starting a Specific Program of Bible Study*

1. What are the four basic types of *Bibles* (not versions)?

2. What is a comparative Study *Bible?*

3. Discuss the benefits of studying the *Bible.*

4. Discuss issues or problems you would like to have answered.

5. List and discuss topics you can research in the *Bible* that would provide answers to your issues or problems.

6. Review and discuss the topics found in our book, *What Does God Say?*

7. Why is preparing the area where You will meet with God important?

Chapter Four – *Studying a Subject in the Word of God*

1. What is the difference between reading the *Bible* and studying it?

2. Why did Jesus speak to His disciples and to us? What did He tell us that we have in Him? (John 16:33)

3. What is "rightly dividing the Word of Truth?" (II Timothy 2:15)

4. Why is studying the *Bible* of great value to your brain?

5. Discuss the difference between how Jack studied the *Bible* and how technology has streamlined *Bible* study today.

6. What is one reason that you need to know the *Bible?* (Matthew 24:24)

7. Will you commit to turning off the television, the computer, or any other device that feeds your brain and your spirit anything that does not honor Jesus Christ? Discuss. (II Corinthians 13:5)

Chapter Five – *The Heavenly City of New Jerusalem*

1. What is the value of carrying with you three by five cards with Scripture verses written on them?

2. Why are we instructed to meditate on God's Word day and night? (Joshua 1:8 -Jack's favorite verse)

3. Discuss the times during each day that we can meditate upon God's Word.

4. What unlocks the door to success in our lives? (Psalm 119:92-93, 177; Matthew 6:33)

5. What is the importance of reading God's Word before we go to sleep?

6. What is the bridge between studying God's Word and acting on God's Word?

7. Explain "meditate on God's Word."

Chapter Six – *Meditating on the Word of God*

1. Why are you instructed to guard your heart? (Proverbs 4:23)

2. What is one work of the Holy Spirit regarding God's Word? (John 14:26)

3. Why does God tell us to "store up" His Word? (Psalm 19:8; Probers 2:1-2)

4. Give examples of God's emphasis on learning His Word. (Deuteronomy 11:18; Proverbs 4:4, 20-21; 7:2-3)

5. Where is the best location for the Word of God? (Colossians 3:16)

6. What is a key to life? (Proverbs 4:7, 23:15)

7. How do you renew your mind? (Psalms 37:31;

Proverbs 3:12)

Chapter Seven – *From Our Hearts to Our Mouths*

1. What reflects what is in your mind? (James 1:26)

2. What promise does God give us concerning His Word? (Isaiah 55:11)

3. (Place this verse on a three by five card and write it upon your heart.)

4. Discuss the primary characteristic of the kingdom of God. (I Corinthians 4:20)

5. Who is the Chief Cornerstone? (Ephesians 2:19-22)

6. What are the requirements for salvation? (Romans 10:8-10)

7. What is another reason to commit God's Word to your heart (I Peter 3:15)

8. Go through the verses and explain the way to salvation in Christ Jesus. Write these verses on three by five cards. Carry them with you. Be ready to speak of the presence of Jesus Christ in your life and how God has provided salvation for all who will come to Him. (You don't need all the verses. I have provided these verses for a clear picture of salvation.) (Acts 16:30b-31; Romans 3:23; 6:23; Ephesians 2:8-9; II Corinthians 5:21; John 1:12; I John 5:13)

Chapter Eight – *Judy's Bible Study Methods*

1. Where in the *Bible* are you instructed to teach the Word of God to your children? (Deuteronomy 6:6-8)

2. What are some *Bible* programs you can use to study the *Bible* online?

3. What is the value of reading a chapter of Proverbs each day?

4. How do the Psalms exercise your emotions?

5. What is an acrostic Psalm?

6. What were the last instructions that Jesus gave to us before He returned to heaven? We'll review this verse again! (Matthew 28:18-20)

7. Why does God instruct us to feed the poor? (Proverbs 19:17)

Chapter Nine – *The Final Step – Obeying God's Instructions*

1. What is a primary verse about filling your heart with God's Word? (Deuteronomy 30:14)

2. What are God's instructions regarding meditating day and night on God's Word? (Joshua 1:8-again-and I Kings 2:3)

3. When you are in Christ Jesus, where are you actually sitting? (Ephesians 2:4-7)

4. Where is your citizenship if you are a child of God in Christ Jesus? (Philippians 3:20)

5. How does God do exceedingly abundantly above all that we ask or think? (Philippians 3:20-21)

6. What do we do to find and live in freedom? (John 8:31-32)

7. What do we do to abide in God? (I John 4:13-16)

The Most Important Question You Will Ever Answer:

———◆•◆•◆———

Have You Entered the Kingdom of God?

You have just read a complete summary of what God says about studying His Word. These are instructions that our Father has written for His children – those human beings who have entered into His kingdom. I ask each reader of this book, "Have you entered into the kingdom of God?"

Jesus Christ said, "...Verily, verily, I say unto thee, except a man be born again, he cannot see the kingdom of God." (John 3:3) Jesus went on to say, "...ye must be born again." (John 3:7) It is very clear that there is only one way to enter into the kingdom of God and that is to be born again.

We don't enter into God's kingdom by church attendance, by teaching Sunday School, by baptism, by confirmation or by living a good life. Jesus Christ paid the price for every one of us to enter into God's kingdom, but this is not "automatic." Many people are so caught up with their own religious denomination or their own personal beliefs that they completely miss God's specific instructions as to how to enter into His kingdom – for the rest of our lives on earth and also for eternity in heaven.

In order to become a born-again Christian, we first of all must admit that we are sinners (Romans 3:23, James 2:10).

We must admit that there is absolutely no way that we can enter into God's kingdom based upon our own merits. Next, we have to genuinely repent of our sins. (Luke 13:3, Acts 3:19) Stop, turn away from them.

After this admission of sin and repentance, there is one additional step that must be taken in order to become a born-again Christian. "For if you tell others with your own mouth that Jesus Christ is your Lord, and believe in your own heart that God has raised Him from the dead, you will be saved. For it is by believing in his heart that a man becomes right with God; and with his mouth he tells others of his faith, confirming his salvation." (Romans 10:9-10, TLB)

Many people know that Jesus Christ died for our sins. However, knowledge is not enough. Intellectual agreement is not enough. In order to be born again, we have to accept Jesus as our Savior in our hearts and not just in our heads. We're not born again until we come to Him as admitted sinners and trust Him deep down in our hearts as the only way that we can enter into the kingdom of God. God knows exactly what we believe deep down in our hearts (I Samuel 16:7, I Chronicles 28:9, Hebrews 4:13). Do you know the joy of having Jesus Christ living in your heart?

We must believe in our hearts that Jesus Christ is the Son of God, that He was born of a virgin, that He died on the cross to pay for our sins, that He rose again from the

The Most Important Question You Will Ever Answer

dead and that He lives today. In order to be a born-again Christian. Romans 10:9-10 tells us that we must not only believe this in our hearts, but we also must open our mouths and tell others of this belief. This confirms our salvation.

When you believe this in your heart and tell others of this belief with your mouth, then you are a born-again Christian. All of us were born naturally on the day that our mothers gave birth to us. We must have a second birth – a spiritual birth – in order to enter into God's kingdom. "For you have a new life. It was not passed on to you from your parents, for the life they gave you will fade away. This new one will last forever, for it comes from Christ, God's ever-living Message to men." (I Peter 1:23, TLB).

God wants us to come to Him, not as intellectuals, but as little children. God does not reveal Himself to us through our intellects. He reveals Himself to us through our hearts and in order to enter into His kingdom, we must come to Him as little children. We may be adults in the natural world, but in the spiritual world we have to start all over. We have to be born again as spiritual babies. Jesus said, "… except ye be converted and become as little children, ye shall not enter into the kingdom of heaven." (Matthew 18:3, KJV).

Pray the following prayer that will help you show you how to be born again:

"Dear heavenly Father, I come to you in the name of Your Son, Jesus Christ. The *Bible* says that if I believe in my heart and confess with my mouth the Lord Jesus and believe in my heart that You raised Him from the dead I will be saved. I do that right now. Come into my heart, Lord Jesus. I confess my sin and turn away from it. I thank You for shedding Your blood for me, so that I am forgiven. I thank You that You are coming back for me. I choose to surrender my life to You right now. Thank You that I am now born of the Spirit. Amen."

You have a mind. You live in a body. Now you are born of the Spirit. "Therefore, if any man be in Christ, he is a new creature: old things are passed away; behold, all things have become new." (II Corinthians 5:17 KJV).

Please tell me if you have come to know Jesus Christ through this or one of our books. That is such a magnificent gift that you can give to me (lamplightmin@protonmail.com)

Now, you must find a church that is centered upon Jesus Christ and the *Bible*, be in the *Bible* every day, and talk with God all day long. Cultivate friends who cause you to grow in Christ Jesus. Go through this book and take notes on how to walk closely with God. You have an excited life that God has planned for you!

We have written 32 *Bible*-filled books to help you in your walk with God in Christ Jesus. Lamplight Global University will provide all our books to you for free. You can grow in our Lord Jesus Christ by progressing through each book, learning what God says about how to live in the Spirit. We invite you to enroll in Lamplight Global University and receive a practical, biblical education. See our website for details: https://lamplight.net

Jack and I spent 30 years writing the books together. Now I am updating our books and he is still co-author with his residence in heaven!

"For God so loved the world, that he gave his only begotten Son, that whosoever believeth in him should not perish, but have everlasting life." (John 3:16, KJV).

Lamplight Ministries, Inc.
1991–Today

The heart of Lamplight Ministries, Inc. is to impart the living gospel of Jesus Christ to every person in every nation. The *Bible*-based writings of Jack and Judy Hartman have reached people in 62 countries that we have on record. Lamplight books have been translated into 16 languages so far. Salvation in Christ Jesus permeates every publication in easy-to-understand language. The focus of Lamplight is how to live victoriously in Christ Jesus and how to do what Jesus said to do: go and make disciples in all nations. Reaching souls for Jesus Christ and making disciples is the heartbeat of Lamplight Ministries, Inc.

Jack Hartman's Need – God's Answer

The ministry began in 1983 when Jack was about to go bankrupt and have a nervous breakdown. A friend told him that if he gave his heart to Jesus Christ and immersed himself in the Word of God, the *Bible*, Jack might not have to go bankrupt.

Jack met Jesus Christ. Jack's life was changed. He searched the *Bible* for everything he could find about finances. He put the verses on three by five cards. He carried them with him. He discovered that God owns everything. Jack also discovered that God's ways are often exactly opposite of man's ways. Jack learned that living to give, giving as a gift of gratitude back to God, is one of

112

God's secrets to receiving God's all sufficiency. God's all sufficiency is God's supply in every area of life, the exact provision needed at the exact time it is needed.

Jack was able to avoid bankruptcy and pay everyone back. People began to ask Jack what happened, so he began a *Bible* study with eight people in an upper room of the Northeast Planning Associates, Inc. office (see https://northeastplanning.com. The *Bible* study kept growing and had to move to the Holiday Inn, then to the Sheridan Wayfarer, and then to the Southside Junior High School cafeteria (Jack remembers getting mustard on his shirt cuffs from the tables). The next location was Memorial High School. Finally, land was purchased in Bedford, NH; Faith Christian Center had a home. A strong mission's program was born as well as a Christian elementary school. The fellowship grew to a thousand people worshiping together on Sunday mornings. Jack was the Tuesday night *Bible* teacher from 1975 until 1989.

Jack was an avid golfer from age 13, when he began as a caddy, to age 81. He made six holes in one!

Trust God for Your Finances **Is Born!**

The notes from the *Bible* study became the book, *Trust God for Your Finances,* published in 1983 (now with over 180,000 copies in print and translated into nine languages). The firm is now under the leadership of Ed Hiers, whom Jack hired when he was 22. The firm, NPA, www.northeastplanning.com, now employs over 100 people-and is an exemplary leader in the insurance industry. Jack mentored advisors on telephone appointments until 2012 and then continued to have select telephone appointments.

Lamplight Ministries, Inc. Is Born!

In 1991 Lamplight Ministries, Inc. was born, when Jack and Judy realized that giving was the core of their publishing company. So many lives were being transformed by Jesus Christ in Jack's books. The ministry was created to allow people who have been blessed by the message of the gospel and the Word of God in the books to be a part of providing more books free of charge, especially to pastors and leaders in Third World nations. Now Lamplight Ministries, Inc. has 32 topical, *Bible*-based books written by Jack or Jack and Judy. The books are a bridge to connect the reader with the Lord Jesus Christ and the living instruction manual, the *Bible*.

Connecting people with Jesus Christ is the focus of Lamplight Ministries, Inc. and subsequently teaching them instruction in righteousness, how to dwell in Christ Jesus and walk with God. The goal, also, is to ignite people to be ministers of the gospel through sharing their faith with others as well as sharing Lamplight books with others.

Jack's Homegoing (July 7, 1931-September 17, 2018)

Jack was absent from the body and present with the Lord on September 17, 2018 with family at his bedside on the last note of the last verse of the song, "Thank you for Giving to the Lord" by Ray Boltz. We picture the last verse with Jesus sweeping his hand around heaven, showing the person all the people who are in heaven because of him. Jack spent his life from age 42 to 88, dedicated to bringing people to heaven and helping them along their journey.

About Judy

Judy is a graduate of YWAM (Youth with a Mission-www.ywam.org) Crossroads Mission Training, where the goal is to know Jesus Christ and to make Him known. Lamplight Ministries, Inc. exists to take God's message of love in Christ Jesus across the world, especially to nations where the spread of the gospel is outlawed.

With a Master's Degree in Secondary Reading, Judy taught in both public and Christian schools. To this day she uses her skills to deliver the Word of God to hungry hearts.

Judy was a founder and director of Ladder Creek Youth Ranch (Omega Ranch) in Scott City, Kansas, where over a hundred young people came to the horse camp each week for free and the counselors trusted God for their finances. Judy is also a John Lyons certified natural horse trainer and is a Level 3-4 in Parelli Natural Horsemanship. She delights in riding horses, playing tennis, kayaking, and organic gardening.

Yesterday and Today

Jack's joy was and Judy's joy is to divide the Word of God into bite-sized pieces in easy-to-understand language. They felt so blessed to have the joy of delivering the Word of God to whosoever was hungry to hear it. Today Judy continues to write *Bible*-based books and to update books that she and Jack wrote together. The books updated with much new content and current applications are *Overcoming Fear, God's Incredible Love for You, Trust God for Your Finances, God's Glorious Eternal Life in Heaven, God's Word on Effective Prayer, and God's Joy Regardless of Circumstances.* These books are waiting for you on our website: https://lamplight.net.

Thousands of books have been sent to the nations over the years. Lamplight continues to ship books to the nations and now provides e-books and audio books as well for pastors, leaders, and all who want to journey in the Word of God. Judy also mentors pastors and leaders through email. Jack's blog is still available! (https://jackhartmans*Bible*teachingsage86.wordpress.com) Stay up to date with Judy's adventures through her blogs: https://lamplightmin.wordpress.com (ministry blog) and https://judyhartman.wordpress.com (biblical health blog). Stay tuned to Judy's current book projects as well as her health and fitness tips that have served her well into her eighties!

Lamplight Ministries Southeast Asia, India and Indonesia

Then Jesus came to them and said, "All authority in heaven and on earth has been given to me. Therefore go and make disciples of all nations, baptizing them in the name of the Father and of the Son and of the Holy Spirit, and teaching them to obey everything I have commanded you. And surely I am with you always, to the very end of the age." (Matthew 28:18-20 AMP) We know that the best way to reach nations of people is through someone from their nation who identifies with them and whom they respect. God knit us together with three men who are now ambassadors for Jesus Christ through Lamplight Ministries, Inc., each in his own nation.

Lamplight Ministries Southeast Asia Director: Dr. Gideon Tandirerung

I (Judy) met Dr. Gideon Tandirerung in 1991. I have known him to share Jesus Christ wherever he is and always start a church for Indonesians and others who speak Indonesian. Gideon knows how to thrive when he is abased and to thrive when he has plenteous provision. He has theological degrees and is certified in the John Maxwell Leadership Training. He is the founder of the Global Gospel Alliance Ministry, is a consultant in human resource development, and is a professor of biblical studies. He is a teacher of pastors and leaders, with doors opening so wide to reach multitudes in Southeast Asia. I observed Gideon's being tried in the fire and that Jesus Christ was in the fire with him. He, his wife, Claire, and their college-graduate daughter, Evangeline are now based in the Philippines, with the goal of reaching Southeast Asia with the gospel of Jesus Christ. Gideon and Evangeline are translating all Lamplight books into Indonesian. Our goal is to print and distribute the books widely on all of the islands where Indonesian is spoken. Gideon's teaching is already reaching hundreds of God's generals, leaders, in His army. We are blessed to have Gideon as our Lamplight Ministries, Inc. Southeast Director.

A Foreword from Dr. Gideon Tandirerung to a Lamplight Ministries' Book

Biblical principles are presented, explored, and expounded in an excellent way for each topic in a topical form. From the hermeneutics or Interpretation approach, Jack and Judy effectively use the *Bible* verses in a very healthy way and in the best way. My former professor, who graduated from Hebrew University in Jerusalem, applied this approach every time he lectured in my class during my theological training. He just brought a unit of Old Testament Hebrew and New Testament Greek every time he taught. He stated clearly to us that the best commentary on the *Bible* is the *Bible* itself. Their books are practical in nature and easy to understand and apply in our daily life-both for new believers or mature ones.

Dr. Gideon Tandirerung,
Lamplight Ministries, Inc.
Southeast Asia Director

Pastor Ebenezer Moses
Lamplight Ministries, Inc. India Director:

I (Judy) met Pastor Ebenezer Moses in 1997 in an appointment designed by God. We each felt directed to a place not of our own choosing, but by listening to a quiet voice inside of us. We met and thus began a knitting of Lamplight Ministries, Inc. and India Gospel Fellowship. Pastor Ebenezer read *Trust God for Your Finances* on the plane ride home to Salem, India in Tamil Nadu. I have been to visit Pastor Ebenezer and India Gospel Fellowship seven times. Fifty acres is owned free and clear with the plan to keep building a community, step by step as funds are available. Pastor Ebenezer has a passion to feed the poor. He did not have a pair of shoes until he was sixteen. By God's grace, he has *Bible* degrees, is an anointed evangelist, and has a heart to reach all of India with the gospel of Jesus Christ. Pastor Ebenezer created the Shepherds Council of India, providing counsel for over 2,500 pastors. He feeds over 250 people a feast each Sunday after church, for many their only meal for the day. Sewing machines are provided for the graduates of the India Gospel Fellowship sewing school. Pastor Ebenezer has translated *Trust God for Your Finances* (copies printed and given to pastors) and *The Rapture and the Second Coming of Jesus Christ* into Tamil. He will continue to translate

Lamplight books. Our plan is to print and distribute them all as we are able. We are so blessed to have Pastor Ebenezer Moses as the Lamplight Ministries, Inc. Director of India.

A Message from Pastor Ebenezer Moses
Lamplight Ministries, Inc. India Director

Jack was and Judy still is a great blessing in my life and ministry. Lamplight books are really light in the darkened path of this earthly life for everyone. The words are very simple and very understandable even to the common men. There is a great famine in the Third World countries for God's Word. Supplying the spiritual food (Lamplight books) free of cost to the pastors of the Third World country is a special and appreciable part of Lamplight Ministries.

Lamplight Ministries, Inc. Uganda Director
Pastor Tonny Ssekyanzi

I, Judy, met Pastor Tonny Ssekyanzi in 1999 when he was sixteen and we began supporting him as an orphan through God Loves Kids (https://godloveskids.org.) We enjoyed meeting with Syvelle and Lovie Phillips at the Missions Conference each year at Countryside Christian Center in Clearwater, Florida, where they represented both of their ministries: Evangel *Bible* Translators and God Loves Kids. We were excited about choosing a child to sponsor through God Loves Kids. We chose Tonny.

Tonny and his three brothers lost their parents in the Ugandan civil war of 1980 to 1985. The four young boys were left in the forest where they lived for three years on roots, fruit and other plants. Lovie Phillips, founder of God

Loves Kids, picked up the boys in the forest and took them to the God Loves Kids Orphanage in Uganda. They had survived from hunger, malaria caused by mosquitos, sleeping sickness caused by tsetse flies, and all water-borne diseases (diarrhea, dysentery).

We have had the joy of seeing Tonny through his education, including a B.A. in Education from the Kampala International University (he had always wanted to be a teacher) and a Bachelor's Degree in Theology from Yesu Akwagala Bible College. (He had always wanted to be a pastor.) Tonny was so thankful to God and to all the people who secured his life that he made the decision to dedicate his life to helping others not to perish, physically and spiritually.

Tonny is now the pastor of Lamplight Church in Kampala, Uganda. He is married to Carolyn and has seven children. (I am happy to tell you that all of my kids love Jesus and know that He is our Savior.) Tonny has translated *Trust God for Your Finances* into Luganda as well as other books.

Tonny ministers to the local people, including providing water for the local families from a well provided through Lamplight Ministries, Inc. While the people receive the water for life's sustenance, they also receive the Living Water of the Word of God for eternal life. Tonny also conducts seminars focused on the Word of God in Lamplight books.

A Message from Pastor Tonny Ssekyanzi
Lamplight Ministries, Inc. Uganda Director

I'm so blessed to be a part of you while serving our heavenly Master. I have been able to minister to the local people and many have been blessed.

Dad Jack was my role model. All my teachings of the gospel to our local people here in Uganda are based on his authored books, especially *Trust God for Your Finances.* For sure, this book covers all my needs, as it has become my light to my salvation and source.

I grew up an orphan and my dream always has been to become a Teacher/Pastor and surely, I kept my dream, lived it and worked hard as a student and it became a reality!! Amen! I am no longer an orphan because I have you as my parents, both physical and spiritual. Thank you for loving me.

I will work along with you to serve God's people through Lamplight Ministries, Inc. This is because you have shown the real truth and faith in God and true mentorship.

Pastor Tonny Ssekyanzi
Lamplight Church
Kampala, Uganda

———————

Our Focus

Lamplight Ministries, Inc. exists to spread the gospel of Jesus Christ to every nation through our *Bible*-based books and our ministry Directors. Our goal is to ignite every reader to become a soul winner and receive a heart to answer God's command to go and make disciples. We chose Lamplight because the *Bible* is a lamp to our feet and a light to our path. (Psalm 119:105) Our goal is to light every heart who reads our books to become a torch for the gospel of Jesus Christ, lighting lives on fire for Jesus wherever they go.

We Invite You to Join our Family

You will bless us beyond measure if you join our Lamplight family by receiving our free monthly newsletter. Go to our website, https://lamplight.net, email me at lamplightmin@protonmail.com or write to us at Lamplight Ministries, Inc. PO Box #202, Harrisburg, NC 28075. I will do somersaults if you will subscribe to our free monthly newsletter! I so want to stay in touch with you! I want to keep pouring the Word of God into you through all our audios, Scripture cards, and books!

You will bless us beyond measure if you join our Lamplight family by receiving our free monthly newsletter. Go to our website, https://lamplight.net, email me at lamplightmin@protonmail.com or write to us at Lamplight Ministries, Inc., PO Box #202, Harrisburg, NC 28075. I will do somersaults if you will subscribe to our free monthly newsletter! I so want to stay in touch with you! I want to keep pouring the Word of God into you through all our audios, Scripture cards, and books!

We invite you to attend Lamplight Global University. You will receive a practical, biblical education through our easy-to-read, biblical books. The price? *Free!* You will learn how to live for Jesus Christ in this troubled world. You will find answers that will make your heart sing! You will get to know your heavenly Father more intimately with each book. Enroll in Lamplight Global University right now!

A major focus of Lamplight Ministries, Inc. is to have our books translated into every known language. Our goal is to print and distribute the books locally in each country. Lamplight books have been translated into Armenian, Danish, Greek, Hebrew, Indonesian, German, Korean, Luganda, Norwegian, Portuguese, Russian, Spanish, Burmese, Hakka Kin, Thai, and Tamil, so far.

We know that God's plan is for all His children in Christ Jesus to use today's technology to reach the unreached with the gospel of Jesus Christ. We will continue to provide free digital downloads of books as well as free audio versions of our books and Scripture cards as well as paperback books for people who have no Internet. Our mission: get people into the Word of God and get the Word of God into people! Jesus Christ is the Word.

About The Authors

Jack Hartman *(July 7, 1931-September 17, 2019)*
& Judy Hartman

Jack Hartman had and Judy Hartman continues to have two passions... their love for Jesus Christ as their Lord and Savior and reaching out to the world and sharing His love and salvation through their ministry of writing and prayer.

Jack Hartman, born in Gloversville, New York in 1931, graduated from the University of Vermont. Judy Hartman, born in San Marino, California in 1939, graduated from the University of Redlands and earned a Master's Degree in Secondary Reading at the University of Northern Colorado. She also attended *Bible* school wherever she lived.

Jack established Northeast Planning Associates in Manchester, NH in 1959 and continued as General Agent until his retirement in 2012. Jack on no medications was "absent from the body and present with the Lord"(II Corinthians 5:8) peacefully and gloriously on September 17, 2019.

Jack and Judy became Health Ministers with MyHallelujah Diet (formerly Hallelujah Acres) in 1997. Their Health Minister code number is #289 out of thousands of Health Ministers world-wide. See https://myhdiet.com. (. You will learn how you can live in energetic health. You will learn that you have a marvelous self-healing body. You can change the course of your health today. Go to https://myhdiet.com now!)

Six children, eleven grandchildren, and four great grandchildren bless Judy beyond measure! Nellie Mae, a mixed-breed puppy, joined the family in 2016.

In her 80's, Judy does not know what the word "retirement" means. She thinks it means re-fire, to touch every life that you can with the love of God in Christ Jesus. Her desire is to reach every people group possible with a translation of Lamplight books which are a bridge for making the *Bible* simple and easy to understand.

Judy and Jan Vail, who have known each other since they were 11 years old, were married on December 31, 2021. At a San Marino High School Class of '57 Reunion in 2018, Jan and Judy began their journey of building Lamplight Secondary School in Kampala, Uganda: Jan, an architect with world-wide experience, and Judy, a teacher who now has an Honorary Doctorate Degree.

Meet Judy at https://lamplight.net and see what Lamplight Ministries, Inc. has in store for you today!

———❦———

Acknowledgments

We thank our heavenly Father for our salvation in Christ Jesus, His Son.

"So, Father, we thank You for sending Your Son to die on the cross for our sins. We thank You that we exchanged our sin for Your righteousness. We thank You that You see us as righteous because of the blood that Jesus shed for us. We thank You that we are children in Your family. We thank You for the joy of living for You. We thank You for the high privilege of delivering Your Word as You direct us. We thank You that You sent the Holy Spirit to reveal Your Word to us. We are so grateful to you, dear Father. We love you so much. In Jesus' name, we pray. Amen."

We want to thank our Lamplight team:

Dan Donaldson, Don Eichelberger, Melissa LaCroix, Mike Hartman, John Wade, and Kim Zinszer for serving on our Board of Directors; Dr. Gideon   and Claire Tandirerung for being Lamplight Directors to Southeast Asia; Pastor Ebenezer Moses and   Sybile for being Lamplight Directors to India; Pastor Tonny and Carolyn Ssekyanzi for being Lamplight Directors to Uganda; to Gail White who served as Jack's secretary from 2003 to 2018 and now serves as Judy's part-time secretary. (https://tailoredpcdocuments.com); Ryan Hobus (https://ctho.com) who has been offering his web design and webhost expertise since 2008; Dr. Ley, our Lamplight proof reader; and Abdulrahman Osamudiamen Suleiman in Nigeria offers his superior skills in preparing our books for publishing. We are blessed beyond measure by each member of our Lamplight team.

We thank God for each of you.

We want to thank our Lamplight Prayer Force and all who pray for Lamplight Ministries, Inc. We know that your prayers make a difference in the lives of every team member and in every life touched by Jesus Christ through our publications.

We thank our Lamplight Ministries, Inc. donors who provide the funds for us to write, publish, translate and distribute our books world-wide free of charge as well as make them available in all the latest technological devices. *We thank God for each of you.*

Lamplight family, we thank you all so very much. You have blessed and continue to bless us beyond measure. We love and appreciate you.

———◆◆◆◆◆———

127

Will You Join Our Team?

Our foremost request is that you pray for us. We request that you pray for our nation, the United States (and for your nation), for the peace of Jerusalem, and for Lamplight Ministries, Inc. at noon each ."The effectual fervent prayer of a righteous man availeth much" (James 5:16 KJV).

Now that we have spent this time together, we want to continue our relationship. We have two blessings for you:

Our free monthly newsletter! To help you grow in our Lord Jesus Christ and gain a world view of God's plan. You will be blessed by:

- Personal news and teachings from Judy

- Monthly mission updates from India, Uganda, and Indonesia

- Teachings from our Directors in India, Uganda, and Indonesia

- Announcements of books and audios added to our website all for free

Lamplight Global University! To train you as a disciple of Jesus Christ and equip you for the specific ministry God has planned for you. If you just want to become grounded in God's Word and know Him more intimately, if you are already in the ministry and want biblical training, or if you are seeking a Bachelor's, a Master's, or a Doctorate Degree, Lamplight Global University is for you!

We have partnered with Victorious Christian Bible University in Lake City, Florida to provide a custom education for you, based on your life situation and your goals.

Go to https://lamplightglobaluniversity.org, study the website to find out if LGU is in God's plan for your life.

So, right now, go to https://lamplight.net and join our team by choosing to receive our newsletter and enroll in Lamplight Global University! You can also email me at lamplightmin@protonmail.com or write to me at Judy Hartman Vail, Lamplight Ministries, Inc., PO Box #202, Harrisburg, NC 28075.

Just in case you missed it! Here's what you need to do right now: go to https://lamplight.net and download the free audio by Jack Hartman himself on How to Study the Bible! Then tell me how much Jack is blessing you here on earth while he is in heaven! I'm looking to hear from you!

Epigraph

"Your word is a lamp for my feet and a light on my path."
(Psalm 119:105 NKJV)

Made in United States
Orlando, FL
22 March 2026

79568207R00085

Early Praise for
Helping You Understand the Bible
God's Plan Made Clear

I have personally been impacted by the writings of Jack and Judy Hartman for nearly four decades now. They have knocked the ball out of the park again with *Helping You Understand the Bible, God's Plan Made Clear*. This inspired book is so timely and needed for this generation. They have compiled their years of study and put it into a simple and straightforward work that is sensational. I have even discovered some new study aids!

In their distinct refreshing, bright, and bold way of communicating the truths of God's Word, I am confident the reader will come away eager about studying the Bible. Following the recommendations in *Helping You Understand the Bible, God's Plan Made Clear* will increase your consecration and faith; it will help you tap into God's divine guidance system and be transformed by His power. I highly recommend this book. It will exhort you, teach you, and bless you.

Dr. Kenneth L. Friendly
Lighthouse Christian Fellowship
Anchorage Alaska
www.lighthousealaska.org

What a privilege it is to be asked to write an endorsement for our dear friend, Judy Hartman of Lamplight Ministries, for this wonderful book, *Helping You Understand the Bible, God's Plan Made Clear*, that Jack composed and Judy is adding to and rereleasing!

Having become a Christian over 50 years ago, by God's grace, I have read the Bible from cover to cover a multitude of times.

Its truths are always refreshing and encouraging, but until you delve into the meat, rather than just the milk of the Word, you are missing so much that God has intended and desires for you to know! His greatest desire for you is a personal, deep relationship, guided by the Holy Spirit that encourages you during the difficult seasons of your life and lifts you up when the world fails you. A daily relationship where He walks and talks with you is worth every effort it takes to attain such a blessed fellowship!

This wonderful resource is a must for any Christian library that gives you step by step instruction on just how to dig deeper into God 's Word and how to retain what you 've learned, so that God 's Word truly becomes a —lamp unto your feet and a light unto your path on a daily basis.

May He direct your steps as you seek to learn and grow in Him!

Rhonda J. Malkmus
Co-founder: Hallelujah Acres, 1992
The Hallelujah Diet https://myhdiet.com

In *Helping You Understand the Bible, God's Plan Made Clear,* you are presented with sensible and practical approaches to Bible Study. Throughout this book, Jack and Judy passionately share the fruit from their years of experience and gleanings from studying the Word. I felt like I was personally sitting with them as they dispensed the treasure of study. My hunger was piqued as I read and reflected on my own pursuit of the Word.

Pastor Brett Robinson
Senior Pastor
Calvary Chapel Palm Harbor Palm
Harbor, FL
https://ccpalmharbor.org